Professional Cheerleading Audition Secrets:
How To Become an Arena Cheerleader for NFL®, NBA®, and Other Pro Cheer Teams

Written by an Industry Expert!

Flavia Berys

Published by

A Division of Cabri LLC
www.cabrimedia.com
Los Angeles County, California

First Printing, 2013

Printed in the United States of America

ISBN: 978-1-938944-01-7

Photo credits:

Author headshot by Richard Pecjak, www.sunset-productions.com.

Book cover photo of the NFL Charger Girl® (wearing blue and gold, with long sleeves) used with the permission of the San Diego Chargers, www.chargers.com. Photograph by Paul Parks Photography. The San Diego Charger Girls are produced by e2k Sports, www.e2k.com. The Charger Girl cover model is Liz Rincon, who cheered for the San Diego Chargers in 2005. She is currently a Realtor in San Diego, California. Her top audition tip is "Above all else, go out there and have fun!"

Book cover photo of the NBA Golden State Warrior Girl® (wearing white with blue and yellow accents, no sleeves) used with the permission of the Golden State Warriors, www.warriors.com. Photograph by Rey Jose II. The Warrior Girl cover model is Patrisha, who currently dances for the Golden State Warriors and has been a member of the team since the 2011 season. She is currently studying Public Relations. Her top audition tip is "To make sure when you audition that you dance full-out, have fun and perform with a lot of energy!"

Book cover photo of the NPSFL Enforcer Girl® (wearing red and black) used with the permission of the San Diego Enforcers, www.sandiegoenforcers.com. Photograph by Michael Manzano. The Enforcer Girl cover model is Alexis Rodriguez, who currently dances for the San Diego Enforcers and is also the team's Dance Director. She works as an Admissions Operations Coordinator. Her top audition tip is "Have fun!"

Pro cheer alumni contributor photographs used with the permission of each respective contributor.

Thank you for your purchase of this book!

As a special **Thank You Gift** to you, you can download some of the checklists and worksheets related to the content of this book as Microsoft Word® and Adobe Acrobat® PDF files for FREE after joining the Arena Cheerleading mailing list. The files can be downloaded and saved to your computer so that you can edit and customize them for your own use!

You will also find extra **BONUS** material such as:

- A video tutorial showing you how to apply arena cheerleader makeup,

- A special report and recipe booklet teaching you how to start your day with better nutrition, and

- Even more bonuses to thank you for purchasing this book!

Please visit **www.ArenaCheerleader.com** right now to join the mailing list and access your FREE gifts under the "BOOK EXTRAS" tab!

Need your help with Amazon!

If you love this book, please don't forget to leave a review at **Amazon.com**! Your review will help make the next edition even better! Every one of the reviews is read, and it really means a lot to get feedback from you, the reader. You can also send a personal email through the website at **www.ArenaCheerleader.com**. Success stories are the best of all!

Thanks again for purchasing this book and good luck at auditions!

Cheers!

About the Author

Flavia Berys is an experienced judge and organizer for professional cheerleading auditions worldwide. The *Wall Street Journal,* Fox 6 San Diego, KFMB Channel 8 San Diego, *Muscle & Fitness Magazine, Woman's Digest, The La Jolla Light* and other media have featured stories about Flavia's involvement in the world of dance and cheerleading.

Her 20-year involvement in the sport includes three years as a UCLA Cheerleader, five years as an instructor for the Universal Cheerleaders Association (UCA), and two years cheering professionally for the NFL as a San Diego Charger Girl before taking her cheerleading career behind the scenes. Flavia coordinated the promotional appearances and transportation logistics for the 2002 and 2003 NFL Pro Bowl cheerleading programs in Honolulu, Hawaii, where she had the opportunity to meet and work with cheerleaders from almost every NFL football team as an Associate Producer for e2k Sports. She was also hired by e2k sports to direct the San Diego Sockers Performance Team, a professional co-ed stunt squad, for two seasons.

Flavia also directed and choreographed the halftime shows for the 2000, 2001, and 2002 San Diego Jr. Charger Girl Programs, and organized and administered a series of youth cheerleading clinics on the island of Guam. She was contracted by e2k Sports to travel internationally to Prague, Czech Republic, where she directed Eastern Europe's first professional cheerleading team, the Eurotel Cheerleaders, which was later renamed the Chilli Cheerleaders. She serves as the executive advisor to professional cheerleading teams such as the San Diego Enforcer Girls in the NPSFL football league. She has worked as an expert witness for trials involving cheerleading negligence litigation, and is the author of other upcoming cheerleading books, *Pom Poms in Prague: A True Story and Professional Cheerleading: A Director's Guide to Starting, Managing, and Marketing an Arena Cheerleader Dance Team.*

Aside from her cheer-related career, Flavia is an attorney, business coach, and real estate broker. She teaches as an adjunct professor at California Western School of Law and San Diego City College. Flavia is available as a motivational speaker and executive consultant. Connect with her at **flavia@berys.com**.

Other books by Flavia Berys

Professional Cheerleading Audition Prep Workbook: A Companion Guide to the Audition Secrets Book

This workbook is a companion guide to the book you are now reading. It is a step-by-step spiral bound workbook that you can use to write down goals, ideas, and to track your progress. It has all the checklists and worksheets you need on your preparation journey. Available at **www.ArenaCheerleader.com**.

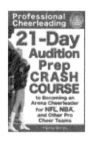

Professional Cheerleading 21-Day Audition Prep Crash Course to Becoming an Arena Cheerleader for NFL®, NBA®, and Other Pro Cheer Teams

This action guide is a companion to the book you are now reading. It is a step-by-step 21-day "crash course" plan that guides you through a short three-week audition prep journey. This is a great book to use when you only have a month or shorter to prepare for the big day! It contains an abbreviated version of the information in the longer book you are now reading, and is designed to give you the best short-term plan to make the most of the limited time you have to prepare. Available at **www.ArenaCheerleader.com**.

Upcoming books by Flavia Berys

Pom Poms in Prague: A True Story

This is the true story of exporting American-style pro cheerleading to the Czech Republic and chronicles the journey of the Czech women who bravely pioneered this new-to-Eastern Europe dance style. Join the **www.ArenaCheerleader.com** mailing list to be notified when it is published. (Coming soon in 2014)

Professional Cheerleading: A Director's Guide to Starting, Managing, and Marketing an Arena Cheerleader Dance Team

This guide will help pro dance team directors navigate the legal, practical, and logistical issues related to arena dance team management. (Coming soon in 2014)

Professional Cheerleading: A Director's Guide to Starting, Managing, and Marketing an Arena Cheerleader Dance Team

This guide will help pro dance team directors navigate the legal, practical, and logistical issues related to arena dance team management. (Coming soon in 2014)

Call Me Atlantis

Fiction (Coming soon in 2014)

The Tangerine Thief and the Concubine

Fiction (Coming soon in 2014)

The Landlord Prep™ Instructional Manual Series for DIY Landlords

Real Estate Legal Guide (Coming soon in 2014)

Legal Notice & Disclaimer

Nothing contained in this book is to be considered medical, legal, or tax advice for your specific situation. The diet and nutrition information in this book has not been evaluated by the FDA and is not intended to treat, diagnose, cure or prevent any disease. This information is not intended as a substitute for the advice or medical care of your own physicians, attorneys, or tax advisors and you should consult with their own physicians, attorneys, or tax advisors prior to taking any personal action with respect to the information contained in this book. This book and all of its contents are intended for educational, entertainment and informational purposes only. The information in this book is believed to be reliable, but is presented without guaranty or warranty. By reading further, you agree to release the author and publisher from any damages or injury associated with your use of the material in this book. Some products mentioned in this book are under trademark or servicemark protection. Product and service names and terms are used only in an editorial fashion for educational purposes with no intent to infringe or dilute such trademarks. If links are provided to specific products, those links are for illustration purposes only and no warranty for such products or fitness for a particular purpose is implied. Such links may be affiliate links that compensate the publisher or author if a purchase is made through such link. Such products are available at a wide variety of retailers and no recommendation is made or implied to use any particular retailer. The opinions of the author do not necessarily reflect the opinions of the publisher.

Contents

Chapter 1:
The Beginning

Introduction

Do you watch professional sports with one eye on the game, and the other on the beautiful, glamorous and energetic cheerleaders?

If you picked up this book, then you dream of cheering on the sidelines at an NFL®, NBA®, or other professional-level sporting event. You love dancing and sports. You have enough enthusiasm to excite hundreds of thousands of fans in the arena. You can't wait to hear the roar of the crowd and dance under the bright lights. You can already imagine what you'll experience as a member of an elite squad of amazing cheerleaders. And you want to make that vision real!

But if you aren't already fulfilling your dream, then you probably have one of two problems:

- either you are someone sitting on the sidelines, feeling too nervous and unprepared to even show up at an audition, or

- you are someone who has already tried out for a pro dance team but was not selected.

If either of those apply to you, I have great news! This book will break down the pro dance team audition process to give you the courage and confidence to show up on the day of auditions, as well as critical success tips to help you get selected. I'm here to help you make it onto the team of your dreams!

I have over 20 years of experience in the cheerleading industry, including two years as an NFL cheerleader, and many years directing professional cheerleading teams in the US and overseas. I have made a career out of training and advising cheerleaders, cheerleading coaches, and pro dance team directors in several professional sports leagues. I have judged at more cheerleading auditions than I can count, and have even been an expert witness in cheerleading-related lawsuits.

Whenever I sit at the judge's table at a professional dance team audition, I know EXACTLY what we look for. I have seen successful candidates do everything right, and other women do everything wrong. It takes so much more than a smile and good dance technique to make it into the big leagues!

It breaks my heart when I see a great dancer have a terrible audition and go home disappointed. I have witnessed far too many qualified candidates get cut at auditions because they didn't have the advice I am going to give to you, and that is why I wrote this book. I will share with you the critical success tips you need to know to properly prepare for auditions. I want you to do your very best on the big day!

While of course I can't guarantee you will make it onto the squad (after all, you might be auditioning against women who have also read this book!), I have made it my mission to give you the training you need to give it your absolute best possible shot.

I WANT YOU TO GO TO AUDITIONS 100% PREPARED AND CONFIDENT! And I will share everything I know to help you get there. This is my commitment to you.

Whether this is your first audition or your 20th, I promise you will find my advice valuable and essential. Some of it may even surprise you. I will share the secrets to image, weight loss, fitness, and beauty that few people outside of the professional entertainment industry know. I will even tackle the uncomfortable topics of racism, ageism, fat discrimination, and cosmetic surgery. Some serious myth busting will take place! Best of all, I will give you a solid action plan to help you achieve your goals.

And the sooner you put my advice into action, the better results you will have on the day of auditions! So let's get started soon.

In the end, I can only tell you what I have learned in my two decades of on-field and behind-the-scenes pro cheer experience; but actually DOING the work and preparing is in YOUR court. So I will teach you what to do and how to get ready, but the courage to put my advice into action and to show up on the day of auditions will come from YOU. And I know you can do it. I really do.

Let's begin!

What's in this book?

This book is divided into sections. The first section is the introduction, which you are reading now. In it, I tell you what motivated me to write this book (spoiler alert: you did!).

The next section, "**Is this sport for you?**," describes why you would want to pursue this goal, what the pro cheerleader personality "type" is in an ideal candidate. I also explore three of the biggest common myths about arena cheerleading.

Next, in "**Your research & advance prep**," I teach you why and how to prepare ahead of time, and what you need to research before the day of auditions.

The next sections are critical, because I will teach you what you need to know to make it onto the squad of your dreams. Those sections are "**Your dancing**," "**Your body**," "**Your grooming**," and "**Your audition attire**."

After that, I tackle the topics of reputation, lifestyle and experience, as well as mindset exercises you can do to help you prepare for the big day. That section is titled, "**Your mindset & self.**"

In "**Your application**," I'll teach you how to make your application stand out.

The section titled, "**Your audition day**," will take you through all of the elements of a typical audition and will teach you tips to help you do your best on the big day.

The last section, "**We are cheering you on!**," contains advice from other alumni pro cheerleaders who want to give you their advice to help you succeed. Like me, they are behind you all the way!

So what are you waiting for? Are you excited yet? Let's keep reading!

Why did I write this book?

The first vision came to me much earlier in my career, over ten years ago, but I put it away in a drawer before it was finished.

Then, very recently, the unfinished book came back to haunt me from its hibernation.

This season, I have already been at three professional cheerleading auditions, either working behind the scenes or as one of the judges. Whether I was advising, assisting the judging process, or serving as one of the decision makers, I had the same thoughts when I saw great candidates go out on the floor and get terrible scores, all because they did not adequately prepare. The thought was, "What a shame! She definitely had potential, but didn't know how to show it off the right way... she's probably not going to make it."

I have a good imagination, so I often see the potential that other judges don't. I work in real estate, and have the eye to see how a "fixer upper" can become a beautiful functional home with a few easy tweaks. I see the same potential in people, both in cheerleading and in my personal life-coaching business.

I see what "might" be, not just what is there in front of me. To me, potential is the North Star that guides us all to the best version of ourselves. When I meet someone, I see his or her best self shine through because I CHOOSE to see it.

I wish all judges had this ability, but the truth is that many don't.

Even so, when I sit as a judge and see unrealized potential in a dancer who is a "diamond in the rough," I need to make the best choice for the team. And that sometimes means turning my eye away from potential when there are better-prepared candidates competing for the limited spots on the team. So even those of us judges who can spot potential won't always take the chance on that "diamond in the rough"!

That's why it's your job to get yourself into the best version of yourself BEFORE the tryout, so that you do not have to hope a judge sees your mere "potential." Make your potential fully realized beforehand, and you won't be taking the chance that a judge will see only what is, rather than what could be.

After being behind the scenes and judging at auditions this season, I got inspired to finish writing this book. I knew it could help a lot of women achieve their dream of cheering on the sidelines at pro sports events. But I knew it would take a lot of work to write this and get it published. While deciding whether to invest the time and energy it would take, I went though my scrapbooks and memory box from my own years cheering for the pros for inspiration. I pulled out photos, videos, handwritten notes from teammates, and other precious memories. I held my metallic gold pom-poms in my hands.

Even though being in the management role today is exciting, nothing compares to those years on the field. I would not trade them for the world. They helped me develop into the person I am today. I have had so many experiences since then, including being in a TV show pilot, appearing in a Sony® video game, being on swimsuit calendar covers, getting through law school, meeting celebrities, interviewing better to land great jobs, being asked to be a public speaker or mistress of ceremonies at events, and so many other wonderful things that were made possible or easier because of my pro cheer training and experience.

When I saw those newspaper clippings, magazine profiles, team photocards, calendars, and other memories—especially the photos of my teammates and cheer sisters—I decided I would do everything in my power to make sure anyone who auditions for a pro cheer squad has the best possible shot at making the team.

But when I think deeper, past my own positive memories of being on my team, and ask myself to honestly face the core reason I wrote this book, I have a series of full-color images flash across my mind. Every image is a candidate's frightened face as she takes the floor in front of the panel of judges.

I see those faces wearing an unforgettable deer-in-the-headlights look, the look of pure terror combined with an expression of disbelief, as if the auditioning woman is thinking, "Is this really happening? This is worse than that nightmare where I show up to school dressed in a Santa suit and everyone points and laughs."

It is no fun to be a judge and see that happen, time after time, knowing the woman will remember her audition experience as traumatic rather than positive.

I want fewer scared, confused candidates, and many, many more confident, radiant faces out on that floor! So let's make sure you are prepared to ensure that you don't feel trapped in a nightmare on the big day!

There are already lots of good books out there to teach people how to interview for a corporate job, audition for an acting gig, or do well at a graduate school interview. It seems that you can find help to prepare for different types of job-seeking situations. But there were no great books on preparing for a professional cheerleading audition, that is, until I wrote this one! That's why I felt this mission was important.

I am continually revamping, updating, and reworking this book to make it as useful, relevant, and easy to digest as possible. Before you read any further, please join my mailing list at **www.ArenaCheerleader.com** so that I can notify you if this book is updated or revised. I also send my mailing list relevant news and information about the arena cheerleading industry. I want you to always have the latest and greatest information! My gift to you is to share my knowledge and advice. That is why I wrote this book!

Why did I want to become an arena cheerleader?

For every one of us who goes down the path to becoming a professional arena cheerleader, there is a story. A spark. A beginning. The initial inspiration. It is different for everyone.

For me, it was in high school. I had danced for years, taking jazz, ballet, tap, and Spanish dance (yes, with castanets!) at a small studio called the West Coast Ballet Theater. My dance teacher, Patty Hoffman, was the owner of the studio and always encouraged her dancers to continually shoot higher and continue to develop our skills.

Her encouragement and training gave me the confidence to try out for my high school's dance & drill team, and later my high school's varsity cheerleading squad. I was the captain of each team, and loved every minute of it. Those were my first experiences with being part of a cheerleading team.

My high school had a community service program and fundraiser arranged with the NFL's San Diego Chargers. Students could volunteer for an evening and work in the concession booth, selling hot dogs and sodas to sports fans. Instead of being paid, the money would go to a non-profit cause. I volunteered to participate one night.

After hours of serving hot dogs, drinks, pretzels, and other concessions to hungry fans, I took a short break to get some air and clear the grease from my lungs. I headed out to the stands, to get a glimpse of the field. This was my first NFL game; I had never attended another live professional sports event before. We had been cooped up in the concession booth since arrival, so I wanted to see what all the fuss was about.

To this day, I remember exactly what I saw. I happened to peek my head out just when the music came on and the cheerleaders on the field began to dance a routine. I was mesmerized. Even from so far away, I could see them clearly. Their gold metallic pom-poms glittered in the night-game lights. I could see their smiles and feel their energy. When a cheerleader's face appeared on the huge screen, I was captivated by how much fun she appeared to be having. Compared to my high school cheerleading experiences, which I loved, what I saw on the Chargers field looked like a million times more fun and exciting.

That's the moment when I set my goal. I knew I would dance on that field one day, wearing blue and gold, with metallic poms in my hands. I wanted to be the person on that screen, sharing my energy and enthusiasm with the tens of thousands of fans in the stands. That was the moment my dream was born.

What was your moment? When did you decide this experience is one of your goals? And how hard are you willing to work to make it happen?

Chapter 2:

Is This Sport For You?

Why should you want to become a professional cheerleader?

There are so many reasons to go down this road. The main reason is that no one should ever have avoidable regrets on their deathbed. If this is one of your dreams, then you owe it to yourself to give it your best shot! Avoid being disappointed years from now, kicking yourself for not even trying. If that reason is not enough motivation, read the list of other great reasons to try out below. And this list is just the start!

Fun & Excitement

Imagine the energy that radiates down onto a sports field or court from the fans in the stands. It is pure airborne adrenaline. When a crowd roars, you feel it in your bones. When your team scores live right in front of your eyes, your heart pumps faster and harder than you will ever feel sitting at a desk or on a coach. When a young child smiles shyly at you at an autograph signing and you see the admiration in his or her eyes, you feel the weight of responsibility for being a role model settle proudly on your shoulders.

There is a reason that professional sports form such an integral part of our society. In every part of the world, people form communities around sports. We watch our heroes on the field and on the court do amazing things and defy the laws of physics and chance. Impossible things happen in sports, like three-point shots that find the hoop or touchdown passes that seem guided by invisible hands mid-air.

The magic of professional sports keeps us glued to our screens when watching from home, and fills us with even greater energy when we attend live. The only thing more exciting than being a spectator is the feeling of being on the field or court with your heroes in person.

As an arena cheerleader, you will have more fun and feel more excitement than with almost anything else you do in life. That's purely my opinion, of course, but I know many, many, many alumni professional cheerleaders who feel the same way. Fun and excitement should not be the sole reasons you choose this path, but they make the ride that much more amazing!

Glamour

Glamour is hard to come by in our everyday life, unless you are a celebrity or royalty. The reason why proms, weddings, and black-tie parties are so popular is in part because we get to dress up for those events. We get to step outside of our "normal" attire and our "everyday" activities to do something magical for a night. It's not just about the dress, or the hair, or the makeup, but about the feeling we get from grooming ourselves into a more glamourous version than we typically see in the mirror every morning.

There is no doubt that professional cheerleading is a glamorous sport. The photo shoots, bright lights, on-camera video opportunities, promotional appearances, and autograph signings will make you feel like a celebrity. Your role will give you plenty of opportunity to find the most glamorous version of yourself and to put that glamorous you out there for the world to see.

Camaraderie & Friendships

Cheerleading at all levels, from the youngest squads to the professional leagues, creates small families of cheer sisters who bond tightly to each other with the glue of shared experience. You will create some of the best friendships you will ever have when you make it onto an arena dance squad. Together, you and your teammates will create magic on the field or on the court. The bonds you form in the process are truly priceless. Even if there was nothing else motivating you to cheer professionally, doing it for the camaraderie and friendships would be enough to make this one of the best things you have done in life.

Contacts & Networking

Although part of you will want to cheer professionally forever, the obvious truth is that you must eventually move on to other things. Your days on the field or court pass by quickly (which is another reason to get started sooner rather than later!) and life will carry you in new directions. The experience of cheering for the pros will help you create professional contacts that can help you in your career.

The contacts you make while on the team can help you network later in life, whether for career or personal reasons. You will meet people who work for team sponsors, the media, local businesses, and within the sports organization itself. Don't forget your teammates, too. Many of your cheer sisters will move into careers that are aligned with what you do or want to do, and cheer sisters love nothing better than helping another sister out!

Here's a great way to open a telephone conversation with a contact made during your time cheering:

> *"Hi Jane, my name is Jenny and we met a few years ago when I was cheering for the [Team Name] and you were our sponsor liaison with [Sponsor Company]. Thanks again for all that you did for the team! We loved the [sponsor product]. Do you remember me?...[Small talk briefly]... The reason I called today is because I'd love your advice about getting into [industry]. I'm [looking for a career change / graduating from school / getting back to work after my kids have grown] and a job in [industry] sounds like it would be a good fit. Do you mind chatting with me for a couple of minutes about the general industry and the opportunities you know of out there that might be a fit?"*

Resume Building

Even if you never utilize your network of contacts (which of course you should!) you will still benefit from listing your time as a pro cheerleader on your resume. Even in conservative professions, this tidbit on your work history can be the spark that makes you stand out from your competition!

When I was interviewing for my first attorney job out of law school, my time working in the cheerleading and dance industry was proudly listed on my resume. What do you think the other attorneys would want to talk about during my interviews? My time working with the NFL, of course!

I was overjoyed when I received a job offer to work for one of the world's largest and most prestigious law firms. The firm I worked for does a lot of legal work for the ownership of some of the country's biggest names in sports. I can't say for sure whether I would have gotten the job if I had left my cheer history off my resume, but I suspect it played a role, whether consciously or unconsciously in the mind of the lawyers who interviewed me. Did my experience with the world of pro sports help my chances and make me stand out as an applicant? I think so!

Here's how your cheer experience can look on your resume. Feel free to tweak and customize the ideas below, which are just a guide to get you inspired. Then prepare to be asked to elaborate during your interview, because this line item from your resume is sure to come up!

If you list your experience under "Employment":

NFL Cheerleader for the Yourtown Teamname, April 2010 through February 2013.

- Spent three seasons as a professional dance team member with two of those seasons as a Team Captain.

- Was regularly selected for media appearances such as news broadcast interviews and local television sports shows.

- Served as a motivational speaker at Eventname, an annual youth leadership event attended by over 500 high school students.

- Participated in autograph signings and team promotional appearances.

- Interacted with fans as an ambassador of the Teamname organization.

- Helped raise over $20,000 through the Teamname Cheerleaders junior cheerleader fundraiser event.

- Assisted dance team management with rehearsal coordination and on-field logistics.

If you list your experience under "Community Service":

NFL Cheerleader for the Yourtown Teamname, April 2010 through February 2013

Participated in fundraising and support for charitable causes as a member of this elite squad of professional dancers. Helped raise over $20,000 through the Teamname Cheerleaders junior cheerleader fundraiser event. Made promotional appearances at over 45 charity events during three-season tenure.

If you list your experience under "Hobbies & Interests":

NFL Cheerleader for the Yourtown Teamname, April 2010 through February 2013

Three-season member of this elite squad of professional dancers. Cheered on the sidelines at all home games, served as an ambassador of the Teamname at promotional events, and participated in charity fundraiser appearances.

Media Training

Before becoming an NFL cheerleader, I did not have any formal media training. Once I made the team, the team director made sure we were all prepared for whatever media opportunity might come up.

This meant practicing answers to common interview questions. It also meant practicing our public speaking and getting comfortable in front of a video camera or an audience. Holding a microphone properly is a learned art, not instinctive. Knowing how to rephrase a question as part of your answer is not intuitive or natural, but many interviewers need you to respond that way. Being aware of your nervous tics, like picking your cuticles or saying, "Ummm," is also a necessary step to mastering media appearance skills.

After your time on the team, all of this training, practice, and experience will prove invaluable to you later in life. How many people receive that kind of schooling? Very few. You will be one of an elite group of people who are prepared and skillful when it comes to impromptu on-air and public speaking opportunities.

During and after my time on a pro team, I have been on the news, been a public speaker, been a law school professor, been a college professor, been an MC (mistress of ceremonies) at charity galas, and even been a Hollywood TV show pilot hostess. Did my journey as a pro cheerleader make these things easier? You bet!

Media & Entertainment Opportunities

You won't just get media training as an arena cheerleader, but you might also be offered opportunities to be in commercials, films, or live events as a result of your experience and contacts in the pro cheer world. During my own time cheerleading, I was on local television numerous times, was on an MTV clip as a dancer, was filmed at Sony studios to play a cheerleader in a football video game, was in a national television commercial, and got to fly around town in our local news helicopter. I have photos of exciting celebrity meetings, and clippings of the times I have appeared in *Muscle & Fitness Magazine*, the *Wall Street Journal*, and other publications. A good friend of mine got to play the local news weather anchor based on her pro cheer background; another cheer-sister is now a popular country music singer out of Nashville; yet another became one of the models on the hit reality game show *Deal or No Deal*. Where will your cheer career take you? You never know where this road might lead!

Confidence Building

There's nothing like accomplishing a goal to get you fired up about your life. When we achieve things, we feel a confidence boost. That confidence will then take us to even greater heights. Confidence will permeate your entire being. The lift you feel when you find out you made the team will create a glow that others will see in your face and in your every move. It lasts a lifetime.

Personal Growth & Achievement

One of the best reasons to become an NFL, NBA or other pro cheerleader is for the feeling of success you will have. That feeling will glow through you, and will light you up from within. We are all capable of accomplishing anything we dream of in life. When you prove that notion to yourself by attaining a lofty goal, your soul will rejoice.

Auditioning for the pros is a brave, scary, and exhausting endeavor. It takes incredible courage, and I honor you for diving in to this challenging journey. By facing your fears, your demons, your insecurities, your doubts, and your ghosts, you prove that you are the kind of person who takes life by the horns. Whether or not you are selected for the team, you are truly remarkable for subjecting yourself to the experience. You should be very proud of that personal achievement!

I know I am proud of you just for reading this book. And when you get out on that floor, please know that I am proud of you from afar, wherever I might be, even if we never meet in person. Whenever I see faces out on an audition floor dancing their hearts out, I'm so proud of my cheer-sisters and cheer-sisters-to-be, regardless of the outcome, regardless of whether this is their year or they must wait to re-audition the following year. I am proud of you just for saying "yes!" to that little voice in you that asks, "why not?"

The key to joy is living your life ALIVE and always taking actions towards your goals, even if just gradual baby steps. Getting off the sidelines is challenging, but it is the only way to truly grow as a person. If you keep moving towards your dreams every day, you will have a better life than most and will find happiness no matter where your life takes you.

Are you the ideal pro cheerleader "type"?

People are great at stereotyping. This is an unfortunate fact. It causes lots of problems when stereotyping leads to intolerance, prejudgment, discrimination, or hate crime. Some social scientists explain that stereotyping is human nature and was originally a good thing, a throwback to our ancestors who lived off the land and had to learn which plants to avoid and animals to hunt based on how they look relative to other plants eaten and animals killed.

Good or bad, stereotyping leads to interesting consequences in our modern age. In the world of cheerleading, there are some stereotypes that have attached themselves to society's perception of the girls and women who choose this sport: "Cheerleading is not a sport," "Cheerleaders are not athletes," "Cheerleading is about looks and not skill," "Cheerleaders are stuck up," "Cheerleaders aren't very smart," "Cheerleaders are beauty over substance," "Cheerleaders are picked solely based on how cute they are," "Cheerleaders are all blonde, tall, fake and clueless," "Cheerleaders try out just to meet the players," or "Cheerleaders are promiscuous."

The best way to fight these stereotypes (which fortunately are not true!) is by example. The more the world sees smart, successful, unique and personable cheerleaders taking the stage, the faster we can defeat and change these misconceptions and assumptions. Luckily, not all people misjudge cheerleaders. But because some people do, we should try even harder to be the role models and leaders that society needs us to be!

While it is not good to subscribe to common stereotypes, there are some qualities that successful pro cheerleader candidates tend to possess. I will go into the main qualities below. When you ask yourself whether pro cheerleading is for you, consider your answers to the following:

Do you love sports?

Cheerleaders dance at sporting events. Although there is plenty of opportunity for promotional, charity, and media appearances, the main duty of a pro cheerleader is to support the sports organization and support the team's efforts on the field or on the court. Ask yourself, "Do I love and enjoy sports and sporting events? Am I willing to learn more about the rules, history and background of the sport? Do I enjoy the game experience?"

Do you have dance training?

Cheerleaders are skillful and talented dancers. For most people, this requires training. Ask yourself, "Do I have the training to dance professionally among skilled dancers? If not, am I willing to get the training and invest my time and money in dance lessons in order to bring myself to the level of skill needed?"

Do you have a "team" attitude rather than a "me" attitude?

Cheerleaders work together as a team, not individuals. Individuality is important, but teamwork is the key to a successful squad. If someone wants only personal fame, she will not make a great teammate because she will be looking out for her own interests and advancement rather than the team's welfare.

In a team of 30 women, imagine if all 30 of them wanted to be the calendar cover model or in the front row of the dance routine! What a nightmare, right? Hurt feelings, resentment, and cattiness would be sure to result, not to mention how difficult the season would be for the team director!

To be on a successful team, all team members must put their personal motivations aside and act in the best interest of the team. There's no room for divas on a pro dance team.

Ask yourself, "Am I willing to put aside my own personal advancement for the good of the team as a whole? Will I be gracious and positive if a teammate is selected for an opportunity that I was not offered? Can I be happy as a part of a team unit, at the expense of giving up any selfish motivations I might unconsciously have in my heart?"

Are you physically fit and athletic?

The sport of cheerleading is physically demanding. You must have the grace of a ballerina, the power of a gymnast, the stamina of a marathon runner, and the energy of that never-stopping Energizer® rabbit. Game days can be long and grueling, especially because a cheerleader's duties begin with rehearsal, promotional appearances, and other events prior to the game's start time. The hours and hours of action, coupled with the short bursts of intense energy during dance routines, demands that all team members be in excellent physical shape.

Many women who audition for pro teams are not in the condition required for the season, and that kind of fitness cannot be obtained overnight. For many tryout candidates, it is this lack of fitness that keeps them off the squad. Either their stamina was poor so that they did not dance their best at the audition after the long hours of learning the routine, or their lack of fitness was evident in the lack of muscle tone and overweight appearance. If a judge sees that someone is out of shape, he or she knows it is not safe or appropriate to put that person in a position where athleticism is absolutely necessary.

Ask yourself, "Am I in the best shape I can be in? Do I have the stamina and strength of an athlete? Does my body look toned and fit or does it betray the fact that I am too sedentary? Am I medically fit to exercise at high intensity levels for prolonged periods? Have I asked my doctor if it's OK for me to become a professional dancer? If I'm not at my best now, what am I willing to do and sacrifice to get in better shape?"

Do you have a polished look or are you interested in getting more polished?

Are you a yoga-pants-and-ponytail girl or a fashionista? Do you find it enjoyable and fun to spend time getting ready to go out? Or do you find primping a hassle? Do you enjoy putting together outfits and makeup looks? Or are you more the kind of woman who thinks less is more and doesn't even own a hairdryer? In other words, do you tend to be a "plain Jane" or a "style coquette"?

Neither is better than the other. I'm personally more of a nature girl, and my favorite outfit is jeans and a tank top with flip-flops. This worked out well for me living in San Diego, which is a surf and beach town, and also when I lived in the Silicon Valley area, where almost everyone was in engineering and thought that khakis and a polo shirt with your company's logo on it made you "well dressed." Even as a lawyer for a large law firm, the office I worked for had a "denim Friday" policy, which I loved. But of course, I'd pair my Friday jeans with high heels and a cute top or blazer, not flip-flops!

Be aware that personal style preference must give way to career and other obligations. If my law office had required that attorneys wear business suits every day, I would have complied. After all, we make these kinds of sacrifices every day. If you work for certain restaurants or stores, you wear a uniform. When you work in construction, you wear a hardhat and steel-toed boots. If you go to school, you follow the dress code. When you change careers, you often have to adjust your attire to your new role, and cheerleading is no different.

As a pro cheerleader, your appearance has to be polished and your level of grooming must meet a higher standard than for most other jobs. Unfortunately, this extends into your personal life because you are in the spotlight even when you are not at a team activity. Family, friends, and fans will know you are a cheerleader for the sports organization even if you are just out at the grocery store picking up a gallon of milk.

So even when off-duty and living your everyday life, you are still expected to maintain a level of professionalism and polish because you are recognizable at all times, not just when on the field or court. What would you think if you saw your favorite local news anchor at the post office and she looked like something the cat dragged in? Or was in curlers, worn out sweatpants, and looked hungover? Like you, a TV anchorwoman must make the same choice and ask the same questions written below.

Ask yourself, "Am I willing to step it up (or keep it up, if already there) with respect to my personal grooming? Will it be a hassle to constantly look polished? How do I feel about being in the public spotlight even on my days off? Do I want the responsibility of representing my team 24/7?"

Are you well spoken with good manners?

Cheerleaders are role models, whether you want to be a role model or not. Other people look up to you, whether it is an aspiring pro cheerleader who thinks of you as a mentor or a young girl or woman who looks to you for general inspiration. If you have a potty-mouth or like to party hard to the point of bordering on "not classy," are you really the right person to serve as that role model? Do you like to speak intelligently, or do you prefer to dumb yourself down to avoid intimidating men or others?

Cheerleaders need to be strong, well spoken, intelligent and kind people. The few who aren't make it harder for the rest of us, so I urge you to do some soul searching before auditioning. Help me improve the image of cheerleading in the public eye by making an honest assessment of yourself. Let's keep the "Snooki" Polizzi and Lindsay Lohan train wrecks out of this sport. If that's your style, consider changing! It will serve you in the long run, far beyond your cheer career.

Ask yourself, "Would friends and coworkers describe me as classy, gracious, and well-spoken? Am I kind and generous to others? Would I make a good role model? If not, am I willing and able to change? Can I make a commitment to become a better person? Do I want positive energy in my life instead of drama?"

Do you have a natural energy that people around you respond to?

Cheerleaders have a natural energy about them that is friendly, positive, and raises the energy level of those around them. When a cheerleader walks into a room, the room's energy should increase, not decrease. People should feel drawn in to that person. The cheerleader should generate energy, and also magnify the energy already in the room, stadium, or court. It takes a particular personality to be this kind of person. It is not a personality you are born with or not born with, it is a personality that a person chooses to have.

All of us can choose how we respond to the outside stimuli in our world. You are the sole captain of your emotional and energetic being. You know those people in your life who are unsinkable? Who have a positive outlook on life? Who make the best out of everything?

Ask yourself, "Am I one of those people whose energy shines the minute I walk into any room? Do my friends describe me as a glowing force of positive energy? Or do I drain the energy from others? Do I generate energy or wait for things to inspire energy in me? Am I a cheer "leader" or cheer "follower"? Can I decide to take my energy up a level or two all the time, so that I am the kind of person that makes others feel better just by being in my presence?"

Do you have enough free time to commit to the game and promotional schedule this sport demands?

The time commitment required to be an arena cheerleader can be daunting. Not only do you have rehearsals and game days, but you must also make promotional appearances. Don't forget to also consider all of your time spent preparing for such events at home, such as hair and makeup primping time.

You do not want to be the team member who is never available for appearances or who misses rehearsals or games. Your other teammates will feel let down and might even resent you. Your team director will be irritated and it may affect your chances of making it back onto the team, or onto another team if another director asks your director about you.

Before auditioning, consider your current work-life balance. Ask yourself, "Do I have the time, or can I make the time, to really commit to being on this team? Can I do this all the way instead of just halfway?"

Are you at least 18 years old?

Most pro dance teams require that all team members be at least 18 years old. This varies from team to team, and I know of one team considering a 21-year cutoff. Be sure to check the age requirements of the teams you are considering in case you are close to this minimum. Some teams will allow you to audition as a minor as long as you reach 18 prior to a specific event, such as the first rehearsal or game.

If you are young, consider whether you are ready for the responsibility and rigors of this sport. Ask yourself, "Am I mature enough to take this role on now, or should I wait until a better time? Do I need more years to grow mentally and emotionally before I assume these responsibilities?"

When are you too old to audition for a pro dance team?

Many teams do not set an upper age limit for their audition criteria. This means that for most teams, you are NEVER too old to try out! For inspiration, you can look up Laura Vikmanis, who made it onto the Cincinnati Ben-Gals cheerleading team at 40 years of age in 2009.

And then in 2012, Laura was almost dethroned from her title as the "oldest NFL cheerleader" by 55-year-old Sharon Simmons, who auditioned for the Dallas Cowboys Cheerleaders but did not make the team. They are both an inspiration to everyone who has ever faced insecurity about age. Age is truly only a number!

If you are an older candidate, don't let age become your wall. Ask yourself, "Do I have the same stamina and skill as a younger cheerleader? Can I keep up with the fitness and beauty requirements of being a pro dancer? Am I willing to work harder than my teammates to make up for the fact that my body might feel a few more aches and pains after rehearsal? Will I make it my mission to look better today than I did at 21? Can I let go of confidence-killing doubts I may have about my age? Can I go out there and rock it with the younger crowd? Am I comfortable knowing that the media might pick up my story and make my journey public? Will I go out there and prove to the world that age is just a number?"

What are the three biggest common myths about looks, body type, and diversity?

Don't let the myths defeat you before you even step through the door. Too many people dismiss the idea of auditioning before they even try because of these myths. Don't base your actions on rumors and false assumptions. Get the real scoop below!

Myth #1: You have to be "model" gorgeous

Truth: Looks matter, but not as much as you might think

A common myth is that a pro cheerleader must have the face and body of a professional model to make it in this industry. That is far from the truth! You do not need to win the genetics lottery to have a future in this industry.

Most people make that assumption because they mostly see arena cheerleaders on the field or in team photocards and swimsuit calendars, where it is true that each cheerleader looks like a professional model. After all, stage makeup, professionally styled hair, and a little Photoshop® action work wonders to make us look flawless on the job!

But in fact, most cheerleaders are transformed into the "girl next door" when they wash off the makeup and pull their hair back into a ponytail. Cheerleaders come in all shapes and sizes. Tall or short, willowy or curvy, brunette or blonde, cheerleaders are some of the most diverse groups of women around!

Never assume you can't pursue this career because of your features or body type. Your looks matter only so far as whether you have made the most out of what you were born with.

Myth #2: You have to be practically anorexic and "skeleton" skinny

Truth: Being skinny and skeletal is not the body-type goal

Professional cheerleaders are professional dancers. Just like any athlete, they are in tip-top physical shape and it shows! That is why you see slim, muscled, toned and strong women out on the field or court. But skeletal women who have starved themselves into a false image of fitness, what I call "faux fit," might look slim and trim, but will not have the stamina and strength necessary to cheer for an entire game day.

To be a professional arena dancer, you will need to be fit, not "skinny." Being fit means you will naturally also be slim and have a low body fat percentage, but it is not the same thing. If you are dancing regularly and maintain a healthy diet, you will achieve the right level of slimness simply because you will be athletic. I call this being "pom fit," which is way better than being "faux fit"!

No team wants to have a cheerleader on board who looks unhealthy, undernourished, and whose ribs are woefully sticking out. There's nothing fun and exciting about watching a cheerleader who looks hungry! So do not aim to be skinny; aim to be POM FIT and that will make you slim enough to make it onto the team of your choice.

If you feel you are not slim enough right now, focus on exercise and diet, not getting skinny. This book contains tips for eating and exercising, which will help you achieve the athletic look you want.

Myth #3: **Teams have "diversity quotas" for minority applicants**

Truth: **Teams do not discriminate by giving or deducting points solely for diversity**

Another common myth is that team directors have specific quotas to fill with dancers from certain ethnic groups. I have heard rumors circulate on many levels of cheerleading—high school, college, the pros—that a candidate's racial background plays a big role during auditions, either by helping or hurting the applicant's chances.

I'm so happy to report that I have not been a part of any audition where there were quotas to fill, and I have never witnessed a candidate being cut based on her ethnic or racial background. Thank goodness! There's enough discrimination in the world already; let's keep it out of cheerleading as much as we can.

I will say that all team management I have worked for or with always express a desire to have a team represent the community, including by reflecting the diversity found in that particular city, town, or state.

The team's management hopes that women of all backgrounds show up on the day of the audition so that the odds of ending up with a diverse team are better. By having a diverse applicant pool, the chances of ending up with a diverse team increases. Nothing is as disappointing as having a pool of 400 applicants, yet not one single candidate shows up from an ethnic group that is heavily represented in that city!

Chapter 3:

Your Research & Advance Prep

Why should you prepare for auditions ahead of time?

The longer you prepare, the better you will do on audition day. This is true for two important reasons:

First, you will feel more prepared and will therefore look more confident. Second, some of the preparation tips in this book will give you better results the longer you do them.

Nothing brings your energy and mood down on the big day than watching all of the other applicants walk in and realizing they look like they prepared for years while you only prepared for days! Avoid that confidence killer.

Keep in mind that some preparation, like taking dance classes, fixing your nutrition, and increasing your fitness level, will produce better results the longer you keep it up. Not only will you dance better, feel better, and look better if you have been dancing, eating right, and toning up for months rather than weeks, but you will feel more prepared and less flustered on the day of auditions.

Some steps take time. If you decide to grow out your hair, as one example, or take dance classes to learn better technique, you cannot expect results in a few days. Well, that's not absolutely true, since this book will teach you about hair extensions and ways to look like a better dancer instantly... but you get the idea!

Some dancers audition many times before being selected for a professional cheerleading squad. It can take a second audition, or a fourth or sixth or eighth, before they make the team. For some dancers, it took them ten years to finally understand what they needed to bring to the floor on the big day. Advance prepping can help cut down the number of times you need to audition before successfully making the squad.

Prepping far ahead of time will also give you the opportunity to try new things with more time to tweak and adjust. If auditions are only a week away, you can't very well experiment with hair colors and cuts the way you could if the audition was a year away. You also can't try new self-tanning creams or tooth whiteners if it is already the week of auditions, in case something doesn't work right. A longer prep schedule gives you more time to experiment!

Hopefully, this book will make that journey of learning as short as possible for you if you read carefully and implement the advice in these pages. And the sooner you get started, the longer you will have to make any necessary changes or improvements before the day of auditions.

Lastly, I believe in visualization and using hard work and focus to bring your dreams to life. By taking a longer approach to your audition prep, you are keeping the goal at the top of your thoughts for an extended period of time. All the time you spend working on yourself to prepare for auditions is also time that you spend visualizing your goal!

My personal preparation story: Learn from my mistakes!

Personally, I did not prepare ahead of time when I first auditioned for an NFL dance team. I didn't research, and I didn't plan ahead.

It might have been out of fear. If I kept my head in the sand, I could force myself to show up that day. I feared that researching and asking around might lead to me feeling inadequate. I also didn't know where to get help, and I didn't want to blindly ask around.

I think I also had a little over-confidence based on my past cheerleading and dance experience. "After all," I must have thought, "I'm a trained studio dancer, and I have cheered and danced through high school, college... I've been teaching dance and cheerleading for a national summer camp organization for several years... what more can I possibly need?"

So I showed up on the day of auditions with little more to prepare me than the information on the team's website and a filled-in application. I remember how my heart thumped when I saw the returning veteran cheerleaders walk in to the audition. It thumped HARD. I also remember the sinking feeling as I wondered, "Uh oh... I am definitely NOT in my element right now." I could have kicked myself for not preparing enough. Except, I didn't want to actually kick myself and tear open my only pair of nylons (you see, I had only brought one pair of hosiery, contrary to the advice I give you in this book on what to pack for auditions!).

I did make it to the final round of cuts before the team was selected, but I was not chosen for one of the 28 spots out of the 400-plus applicants. I vowed I would come back better prepared. I would spend more time on my solo routine, and now knew what to wear (I had noticed all the returning veterans were in jazz shoes, while I was in cheer sneakers with socks!). I took note of hairstyles and realized my college cheerleader half-ponytail was not the right look. I learned that I should wear false lashes to accent my eyes, and that it looks odd when a person's nylons don't match their arm and stomach skin tone. I learned, and I learned, and I learned. Hindsight was 20/20.

But...

Even with all of this newfound knowledge, life got away from me and I was very busy with college and social obligations. My college cheer squad competed nationally, and my focus shifted to that. My graduation was approaching, and my spare time was spent planning for the next steps in life. My dreams of dancing for my local professional dance team were put on hold. I did not take those dreams off of the back burner until I saw a short clip on the news reporting that the auditions for that team were that week. That very week!

I raced around and put together a better audition outfit than the previous year. I shopped for false eyelashes, and tried to figure out how they get applied. I must have gone through two tubes of eyelash glue! I bought a pair of nylons from every shelf, and tried them all on in front of the mirror, but did not have time to dance in each brand. I hastily put together a solo routine in case I made it to finals, and regretted that I had not taken any jazz or other technique classes that year since I didn't need that type of technique on my co-ed college cheer squad.

I arrived at auditions better prepared than my first year, but still very much under-prepared. Again, I was selected for the final round. Again, I was not selected for the team. And deep down, I knew it was 100% my own fault. I had not prepared the right away. I had given it a nice try, but not a good try. Getting cut after giving it my best shot would have felt better, because then I could have at least known I had done all I could to reach my dream.

I did not give up. My third year, I planned ahead and put important milestone dates into my wall calendar. I took dance lessons, and put a lot of thought into what I would wear, how I would look, and what I would bring when preparing for the auditions. In my mind, I visualized myself owning that dance floor on the big day. I even daydreamed about standing on the sidelines at the first big game!

I went to auditions with a completely different mindset. I did many of the things that I advise you to do in this book. Some of what's in this book, I didn't know until much later, when I became a judge and worked behind the scenes, but my performance would have been even better if I had known everything I'm sharing with you.

I made the squad that year, which was my third audition for that team.

There are two lessons here:

First, preparation is key. It will improve your chances more than you can imagine. *Second*, the old saying is true: "If at first you don't succeed, try, try again!" Never give up. Never. Give. Up... Never!

What if I'd given up after the second failed attempt? What regrets would I have lived with? Think about that. If it's worth it to you to try in the first place, it's worth it to try, try, and try again.

What's your most dangerous audition success enemy?

After learning the lessons above, if there's one thing I can tell you, it's that procrastination is the enemy. It is so easy to put things off, especially when the goal is so far in the future. Like writing a term paper, many of us wait until the last minute or until the situation is critical before acting. Don't fall into this trap!

Start preparing now. Don't read this book and make a plan to "someday" implement these tips; instead, take some action today. As soon as you read a tip you can put into action, make a note on your calendar to get it done. Don't procrastinate, or you could find yourself pulling this book off your shelf seven days before the audition. If you do that, you will have a sinking feeling in your stomach as you realize that your results would have been a million times better if you had started earlier. Remember, this is "SELF help" not "SHELF help," okay?

You might be the kind of person who gets things done early and without needing much reminding or outside help from others. But if you are a procrastinator in life, then you will love the workbook I developed as a companion guide to this book. If you don't have it already, order it at **www.ArenaCheerleader.com.**

It is a step-by-step spiral bound workbook that you can use to write down goals, ideas, and to track your progress. It has all the checklists and worksheets you need on this preparation journey. It is organized in the same order as this book, so that each major section in this book has a corresponding worksheet for you to fill in. This might be what you need to stay on track and accomplish your dreams of becoming a professional cheerleader!

Another idea is for you to pair up with a buddy or mentor. Alumni or current arena cheerleaders make great mentors, and a fellow aspiring candidate would be a great workout, dance, and goal-meeting buddy. I'm a huge believer in the buddy system. See if you can find a friend to join you on this journey!

Do you need to be perfectly polished at auditions, or can you just show the judges "potential"?

One of the big misconceptions in professional cheerleading is that you are judged on your "potential." Friends and family will tell you, with good intentions, that the judges can see through bad hair or amateur moves and will envision the bright diamond that someone could become with just a little polish. Is this true? Only partly.

When people show up on a lark with no preparation, most judges assume the person is either clueless, ill-prepared, inexperienced or not taking the process seriously. Often, it is hard to tell if someone was innocently clueless or intentionally careless when she shows up at an audition completely unprepared. Depending on the judge, this can be taken as offensive or casts doubt on your potential. Many judges are celebrities or businesspeople, and they do not respect someone who wastes their time.

It is true that judges will often look through choreography errors or makeup problems to see whether a candidate can be shaped into what the team needs. But assuming this will happen to you is like assuming that you can move to Los Angeles to work as a waitress and be automatically "discovered" by a big-time director when you serve him or her lunch.

It can be a longshot to rely on the judges' imagination (and their forgiveness of your obvious lack of preparation). A far better plan would be to show up looking as close to the "diamond" as possible, rather than taking the chance that the judges will have the creativity needed to envision you as an "after" when you show them only your "before."

Also, you should keep in mind that not all of the judges will have the skills to spot "diamonds in the rough." Often, a professional sports team will include celebrity judges such as local news anchors or TV personalities, or team sponsor representatives, such as the owner of a restaurant chain. Judges may include marketing professionals or team ownership, and many may not have the experience to imagine in advance what you would be like after a makeover.

So where one judge sees your potential, another might see only the rough exterior and unpolished appearance. Remember, you have to impress as many judges as possible to increase your chances of making the team.

In real estate sales, a "fixer upper" is harder to sell than a beautifully staged home. That is because some buyers will not have the imagination to see what the house could be with some new paint, upgraded flooring, and new fixtures, while other buyers will have the imagination, but will lack the desire to do all of that work when the house down the block is ready to move into with no work needed.

Remember, many people would rather take the easy path so they can focus their efforts on other things. Likewise, a dance team director might prefer to spend his or her time marketing the team and on big picture items rather than spending a lot of time on one individual team member's transformation into a better dancer or more polished spokesperson.

The simple truth is that even though makeovers and training can take a dancer from a strong "maybe" to a "WOW," why would the judges and team director pick a diamond in the rough if you are competing against women who have already done the work? They are taking a chance on you if you will need a lot of prepping before you can be sent on promotions and to games. You are a riskier pick.

If you were a judge, would you rather have team members who need a lot of work and polish on your team? What if it turns out that potential was an illusion, and the dancer never improves? And the bigger question in the judge's or director's mind, "If someone does not prepare for auditions, can that person be trusted to prepare for the season, and games, and promotions? I see potential, but is she actually trainable? Does she even care enough?"

Don't make the judge wonder that about you. Show them you already did the work, and you won't have to prove that you have potential. You won't need mere potential when you have the complete package already proudly on display.

What is the main difference between cheering for the NFL vs. NBA?

Besides the obvious difference of cheering for a different sport, many aspiring arena dancers want to know if the dance style and audition styles are different. The answer is: It depends.

This book will address the recommended steps for researching the teams you are interested in. Part of that research will involve evaluating the style and look of each team.

As a general rule, pro football and pro basketball cheerleaders tend to have a similar style. Both types of cheerleading require similar abilities and talents. But on average, football arena dance programs tend to focus on a jazzier, more glamorous style, while basketball arena dance programs tend to focus on a sportier, more athletic style.

The advice in this book will serve you no matter which league you audition for, but keep in mind that every team is different. Part of your research will be to objectively evaluate the photos, videos, and other information about your dream team to see what type of style you should focus on.

Should you consider teams other than NFL and NBA dance teams?

When people think of professional cheerleaders, it's likely that an NFL or NBA cheerleader comes to mind. These are the "big leagues" of this sport, and many dancers aspire to dance for a team in one of those two national leagues.

But what about other professional or semi-pro leagues? Should you consider starting your career on a dance team in a smaller league? Will that hurt or help your chances of transitioning onto an NFL or NBA dance team down the road?

Most importantly, are you even aware of all of the smaller-league options available in your local market?

Do some research to see what your town's pro or semi-pro sports teams are, and look outside of football and basketball. You might discover dance teams that cheer on the sidelines for pro hockey, soccer, and other teams. Baseball, rugby, and other local sports organizations might have sideline dancers as well. Some of these teams may play in semi-professional or club sport leagues rather than professional leagues, but that doesn't mean that you should dismiss the team without first taking a closer look.

Look at their websites, visit their social media fan pages, and see if you can search on Google® for information or videos about the team. See if there is a cheer or dance team, and whether the quality of the team looks good. Identify any of these smaller-league teams you would be willing to dance for if you are not successful in making it onto an NFL or NBA team, or if you decide you'd rather get some in-arena experience on a smaller team before auditioning for the big national leagues.

Many dancers find that dancing for a team in a smaller league is an ideal way to polish their skills and make it into the big leagues after a season or two on a smaller team, so keep your mind open. Others choose a smaller league team because the game schedule fits their personal calendar better, or because the time commitment is less rigorous on one team versus the other.

It is not unusual to have dancers hop around among various local teams from year to year. The beauty of cheerleading is that your career can spotlight multiple teams. I know dancers who have cheered for three, four, or more different professional teams in their career. Sometimes, you can even cheer for more than one team in a single year if the sports schedules do not overlap.

As an example, the cover of this book features a football cheerleader from an NFL team and also one from a semi-pro league, the National Public Safety Football League (NPSFL). Both teams are based in San Diego, California. Both teams have fantastic cheerleading programs. Dancers on the smaller-league NPSFL team have transitioned to the NFL team, and on the flip side, cheerleaders from the NFL team have also transitioned to the smaller-league NPSFL team. The cover also features an NBA cheerleader. I can tell you something that all three of these women have in common: Cheering for their team has been one of the best experiences of their lives.

Later in this book, you will read the advice of many pro cheerleader alumni. If you look at their biographies, you will see that many of them have cheered for more than one team, and in many cases more than one league. Use this as food for thought: Should you consider additional teams in addition to the dream team you have your heart set on? Should you research to see what else is out there?

What do you absolutely need to research before auditions?

Your research checklist should look something like the list below, which you can adjust as necessary for your own goals and geographic area. If you want to download this list in a Microsoft Word® (so that you can customize it) or Adobe® PDF format (so you can print it out), you can download it for free if you join the Arena Cheerleader™ mailing list at **www.ArenaCheerleader.com**.

- **Create a research binder.** This can be either a physical binder, or a folder on your computer if you prefer to go paperless. You might decide to do both, since part of your research will involve gathering printed material. Of course, even magazine clippings and other physical documents can be scanned and saved electronically, so depending on your style, you can make your research binder anything you want. You might even decide to decorate it or create a small box or trunk to store your research and everything that you gather in the process. If all goes as planned, you will eventually begin to add the items related to your new team!

- **Make a calendar.** If you keep and use a calendar already, that's great. You do not need a separate calendar for your arena cheerleading audition preparation. But if you don't, I highly advise you start a calendar to keep track of deadlines, goals, and planning. Even if you keep a calendar for work or your personal life, you might decide to create and keep a separate calendar for your audition prep efforts in order to keep a sharp focus on what you are working on. If you have one particular team that your heart is set on making, why not purchase one of their swimsuit calendars (if they have one) to use as your goal-setting calendar? Now that's inspiration! The only downside is that many swimsuit calendars focus on the photos and have only very small areas to write in. Believe me, you will have plenty to write in this calendar, so pick one that has space for your notes!

- **Research local teams.** Which are the local professional cheerleading and dance teams in your region? As discussed in another chapter, don't stop with just the NFL or NBA teams, keep looking for teams that dance in smaller or semi-pro leagues. You might discover dance teams that cheer on the sidelines for pro hockey leagues, soccer leagues, and other teams that didn't come to mind off the top of your head. Identify the teams you would be willing to dance for, and try to be open to non-NFL and non-NBA teams so that your list has some backups. Many dancers find that dancing for a smaller league is the best way to polish their skills and make it into the big leagues after a season on a smaller team.

- **Research non-local teams.** Which are the non-local professional cheerleading and dance teams in regions you would be able and willing to relocate to in order to dance on their sidelines? For example, you might decide you would be willing to move to Dallas to dance for the Dallas Cowboys®, or that you have always wanted to live in Miami and would love the excuse to move there if you make it onto the Miami Dolphins® dance team. Maybe Los Angeles is your dream town, and the Lakers® are your favorite basketball team. Why not make that team your goal? Consider whether you would be able, ready, and willing to pack your bags for the opportunity to dance for one of your dream teams and add those teams to your list!

- **Compile.** For each team you identify above, visit their web page and print out or cut and paste all relevant info about the cheerleading program into your research file. Create a separate section for each team. The amount of information available might surprise you. You should include the following, if available online:

  + General information about the sports organization, such as where they play and which league they play for. This is probably on an "about the team" page on the main website.

  + Photos of the current dance team, especially the team photo. Many sports organizations create a dedicated subpage for their dance and cheerleading teams.

  + Individual photos of the dance team members.

  + Sample biography pages of the dance team members.

  + Information about dance team auditions, including any handouts or applications that you can download.

  + General information about the dance team, such as how many members are on it and how often they rehearse.

  + Contact information for the team director and/or coach.

  + Information about any team-sponsored dance workshops or meetings.

  + Season schedule, or range of months if the exact game schedule is not available.

  + Watch all videos available on Youtube® or on the team website that showcase the dance team, and make notes about the dance style and level of difficulty noted, such as whether there are double-turns or technical dance moves.

+ Make a note about whether each team uses pom-poms or not. If poms are used, research to see if you will need to use pom-poms at the audition so that you know whether you need to start practicing dancing with poms in your hands.

+ Run a Google® search on each team two ways: First, run a standard search. Then, run an "image" search. Read press releases and articles, and review images that come up on the search. Gather anything you find interesting or relevant about the organization in general, and dance team in particular.

- **Fill in your calendar.** As you compile the information above, enter any relevant dates and deadlines into your calendar. If you are interested in many different teams, it might be helpful to color-code your calendar entries. Enter season start dates, games, audition workshops, audition dates, bootcamp or mini-camp dates, rehearsal schedules, and any deadlines (such as application deadlines). This will help you determine which teams to focus on, since some auditions may occur on the same day or otherwise conflict. You can also see if it is possible to dance for more than one team, if the seasons do not overlap.

- **Contact team directors.** There is a fine balance between being professional or a pest when contacting dance team management. You will want to reach out at a time when there is not a lot of email and phone traffic. The day before auditions or a game is not a good choice, because the team director will obviously be quite busy and will not have time to address your questions. In order to avoid being an unwelcome interruption, choose an off-season time to reach out. It is up to you whether you want to do so by telephone or email. You can try doing both, but beware that it's possible you won't get a response right away. You might not get a response at all, in fact, which will tell you something about whether that director is one you want to work with in the future. I have included some sample scripts below; feel free to deviate from these ideas and insert your own personality. Keep in mind that your tone and the way you come across in these preliminary contacts can affect your chances of making the team in the future. A director will often remember a name or person many months later, and you want that memory to be a positive one that will help you make the team, rather than a memory that will have the director think, "No way I'm having her on my team, I remember her rude attitude." Here are some sample queries:

+ "Hi Ms. Smith, My name is Jane Jones and I am a huge fan of the [City] [Team]. I spent last season with a smaller league team, the {Other Team], and even though it has been a fantastic experience and great training, I feel that I am finally ready to move up! I'm very interested in auditioning for your dance team next season. I took a look at the website for information, but I had a couple of questions that I hope you can answer for me. I want to feel prepared for the day of auditions, so I'd appreciate you sharing with me how many applicants usually audition so that I can picture what it will be like that day. Also, does your choreography tend towards hip-hop or jazz for the audition routine? I have seen that your sideline routines include both, but maybe the audition routine is typically one or the other and that would help me prepare. I respect your time, and really appreciate any response or help you can offer. Best regards, Jane."

+ "Hi Ms. Smith, We met at last year's [Team] audition. I really enjoyed the experience, and even though I was not selected, I'm very excited to come back and audition again this season. I have selected three audition outfits, and am having a hard time deciding which one to wear to auditions next April. If you have time to take a look, it would be really helpful for you to tell me if one stands out to you as more appropriate, since you know what your judging panel looks for. I have been working really hard since last April, and can't wait to show you and the judges how far I have come. Thank you very much for your time! Sincerely, Jane Jones."

+ "Dear Ms. Smith, Thank you for sponsoring the audition clinic this past weekend. I have cheered for four teams in my dance career, and this was by far the best and most comprehensive pre-audition workshop I've been to. The clinic answered all of my questions except one: do you recommend dance sneakers or jazz shoes as footwear? It would be great to know what the returning veterans usually wear, so that I can do my best to blend in with what the existing team members will be wearing. And of course, any other tips or advice you can offer are very welcome. I really want to give it my absolute best shot out there, so that I can be an asset to you and your team this season! Respectfully, Jane Jones."

Now that you have gathered all of the research into your file, you can look through it to decide which team auditions you will focus on this coming season. Analyze the calendar entries to determine how long you have until auditions. Read through this book carefully, and as you get to each chapter, make notes in your calendar.

For example, set a date by which you need to have your audition outfit selected. Decide when you will experiment with new hair colors, try new tanning sprays, and so on, and enter each step into your calendar. This will help you stay organized and will combat the possibility of procrastination. If you start preparing at the last minute, your results will not be as good.

Your calendar will serve as the prompt to get you on track. Every person's calendar would contain different things, so there is no one-size-fits-all. But to give you an idea of the types of things to add to it, see this list below. Your list can include things like:

- "Try new dance classes this week to find best jazz and hip-hop instructors."

- "Make hair appointment this month to try new color and cut."

- "Go through Facebook page and delete inappropriate photos."

- "Find best self-tanner for my skin."

- "Sign up for boot camp cross-training classes."

- "Look through magazines to find good makeup looks."

- "Sign up for Toastmasters® public speaking club."

- "Experiment with ways to cover up tattoo."

- "Start eating better this week; commit to maintaining a healthier diet starting now."

- "Call dentists to find good deal on teeth bleaching; make appointment."

- "Visit mall department store to experiment with lipstick colors."

- "Practice applying false lashes."

- "Need audition outfit by next week."

- "Buy pom-poms online by today to begin practicing dancing with poms."

- "Choreograph audition solo and 8-count this week."

- "Videotape self doing solo routine; bring video to studio and ask dance teacher for feedback."

- "Study football rules this week."

- "Shopping list this week: Hosiery tights, false lashes and lash glue, and new dance shoes."

Obviously, this is only a sample list, but should give you an idea of the things you should calendar so that you stay on track and don't overlook something. You do not want to get caught off-guard racing around town to find the perfect dance shoes the night before auditions. Advance planning is key; it will help you focus on the important things the week of audition, like rehearsing your routine and getting lots of sleep, rather than shopping like a madwoman.

As a reminder, if you want to download this list in a Microsoft Word (so that you can customize it) or Adobe PDF format (so you can print it out), you can download it for free if you join the Arena Cheerleader™ mailing list at **www.ArenaCheerleader.com**. Now, start writing!

How sports savvy do you need to be?

Women often stress about their football, basketball, or other sports rules knowledge before the interview portion of the audition. It is true that many teams will incorporate sports rules knowledge questions into the interview, so you should learn or brush up on the basic rules before the day of auditions.

You will need to know the basics, but not every tiny nuance. Your knowledge level should be that of a team fan who attends many games, not necessarily that of a coach or player.

The best way to learn the rules is to watch sports on television with friends or family and to ask questions during the game. Sports fans love explaining the rules to others because it is a way to show off mastery over the sometimes incredibly complicated rules. If you prefer to study on your own, a book like

Football for Dummies or *Basketball for Dummies* will teach you everything you ever needed to know about the complicated rules for these games!

What is more important, dance skill or appearance?

Judges look for the complete package. Many audition candidates hope that their superior strength in dance will outweigh any weakness in their polish and appearance, or vice versa. But the truth is that both are equally important, and you will be competing against women who have spent time on their own skills to excel in all areas. You should be equally diligent when preparing for auditions.

Do not depend on your strengths to compensate for your weaknesses. It is easy to convince yourself that you do not need to work overly hard in preparing because you already shine in one or more categories. Don't ignore your weaknesses out of denial. Although it will be tempting to focus on your existing skills because it will feel good to sharpen an already sharp blade, get the dull knives out into the open so that you can address and strengthen those areas of weakness.

In my judging days, I have seen many technically breathtaking dancers who did not prepare their look properly. I have also seen perfectly polished candidates who wowed us during their walk out onto the floor and name introduction, but whose lack of dance training was obvious within the first eight-count of music. At a competitive audition with lots of qualified candidates, neither situation bodes well for the applicant.

To be the complete package, you need to prepare ahead of time, even if you are already strong in one or more areas.

Chapter 4:
Your Dancing

Why can a dancer with just one year of dance training "out-dance" a professional ballerina?

Dancing is like any sport; some people take to it easier than others. We are all born with certain skill sets and tendencies. Some of us are musical and can sing beautifully with no formal training; others need years of voice lessons to achieve the same level of talent. Your aptitude for dance is personal to you.

You might have years of dance training, or you might be a virtual newbie to formal lessons. You might be a natural, or perhaps you need major help just to learn to count music in your head. You might pick up choreography with an almost photographic memory, or maybe it takes you twice as long as other dancers to learn a routine.

For any cheerleader, dance training is essential. Even the best technical dancers can improve over time with additional lessons and practice. You should make dance training part of your journey before auditions. The longer you take lessons, the better you will dance. Being in practice also makes it easier to memorize choreography quickly. Many candidates find that audition routines are taught very quickly, and those who haven't been to dance classes in years seem to struggle the most with picking up the moves.

This chapter will help guide you to the type of dance lessons best suited for arena cheerleading.

Why should you choose your dance class style carefully?

Keep in mind that ALL dance training is beneficial. There is not one single moment of dancing that is wasted in your development as a movement artist.

Even your limbo antics at a beach barbecue have value! But while all dancing is good for you, some dance styles are better than others at approximating the most common arena dance styles.

When choosing dance classes, keep the comments below in mind. Try to do at least one style in the "best" list, but feel free to also take classes from the "less than ideal" list. Just because it is not the best, doesn't mean you won't get good training and practice out of it! These lists could have been much longer, but I kept it to the dance forms you most commonly find at neighborhood dance studios.

Above all, I recommend participating in as many forms of dance as you can fit into your schedule and budget. Not only is it good for your audition prep, but it is also fun and great exercise!

Best dance styles for arena cheerleading preparation:

- **Arena dance**. If you are lucky enough to find an arena dance cheerleading class in your town, by all means sign up! This is probably the only dance style that will include exactly the type of dance you need to learn to be a successful arena dancer. The class will even likely include pom-pom work, which is a must-do when preparing for auditions! As a bonus, there is a good chance that the teacher will be a current or former dancer for a pro team that you have your eye on. Double score!

- **Jazz**. If you are only going to take one style of dance to train for your arena cheer career and arena dance classes are not available, take a good jazz class. You will learn the turns, leaps, kicks, and movement that are the basis for many pro cheerleading routines. In jazz dance, you will learn to point your toes and move across the floor properly. This class will teach you the vocabulary and body positions essential to arena dancing.

- **Bellydance**. Bellydance classes are a great way to tone your stomach and loosen hips and shoulders. It's also a great style for working on hand movement and graceful arms. Who knows? You might be the next Shakira! You can even get a DVD to practice this style at home. My favorite is *The Goddess Workout: Bellydance Collection*, created by Dolphina. I know Dolphina personally and have trained with her, and can say with confidence that she really knows how to teach goddesses to move!

- **Latin ballroom styles**. The drama, head position, and flair of Latin floor dances such as flamenco, salsa, and tango are a great way to develop stage presence. These styles emphasize body lines, pointed feet, and precision, which are all great training aids for arena dancing. You will also work on developing high kicks with pointed toes.

- **Hip-hop**. Many arena cheer routines incorporate hip-hop moves into some or all of the team's routines. Hip-hop will help you achieve movement isolation skills as well as flexibility in your spine. Hip-hop's focus on quick and precise movements will build muscle tone and will improve your arm and leg placement. The hip movements will work your stomach and thighs, much like bellydancing.

- **Bollywood**. If you have not experienced the bollywood dance style, please go search online and take a look at a bollywood routine! If you can find a studio near you that teaches this style, you will have a lot of fun as it is usually performed in groups and incorporates quick challenging movements which will work your entire body.

- **Zumba®**. If you are going to take a class at your gym or fitness center, see if Zumba® is offered. This fast-paced, energetic dance style is a great choice for your pre-audition training. Just beware—unlike traditional dance studio lessons, the Zumba® instructor will not take time to critique individual dancers and help coach technique. The instructor is usually there to lead the class as a whole and to make sure everyone is sweating, not to analyze or work on your dance skills.

- **Broadway**. If you have local theater, see if the theater offers any dance classes. The Broadway style is a good one for practicing big confident movement and learning choreography.

- **Disco**. Disco is the king of hip wagging movements that are fun to perform and help you develop a confident attitude in your movement. However, the lack of technical turns, leaps, and arm motions almost made me put this style in the "less than ideal" list. But then I thought about how much value that confidence and sexiness adds to an audition routine, and I bumped disco up because nothing says "watch me" like a well-executed disco routine!

Less than ideal dance styles for arena cheerleading preparation (but still great add-ons as part of a well-rounded regime!):

- **Ballet**. Almost every audition I have judged had at least one classically trained ballerina show up. They are easy to spot. Although a ballerina's toes are pointed tight, and she can showcase flexible legs and graceful arms, I see the same problems over and over when a long-time ballerina takes the pro cheer audition floor. She is usually a beat behind on hitting dance moves, because she floats gracefully into each position rather than hitting the move sharply. She usually lacks power, and her movements are soft rather than punchy. Her kicks are high, but drift up and down rather than scissoring quickly like they need to. Her hips, shoulders, and torso are not sassy when she tries to add some flirt to a dance move. Her face wears a stern and serious expression, as she was trained to do when dancing in Swan Lake and other somber performances, rather than the joyous and energetic smile of a true cheerleader. If you have studied ballet for years, please be sure to expand your dance styles and to get focused coaching to become more versatile. If you can switch from ballet to cheer and back to ballet again at the drop of a hat, that's great. But if you come out on the pro cheer audition floor with the grace of a swan, you will look too soft when measured against the other candidates.

- **Modern**. Modern dance is similar to ballet in its softness of movement. It is a gorgeous style, but many of the issues I see in ballet dancers also come up when a modern dancer takes the floor. Because modern dance has fewer rigid rules and positions, most modern dancers can make the switch to jazz, bellydance or hip-hop fairly easily.

- **Fitness aerobics**. Every once in a while, a fitness aerobics expert shows up at an audition. I once witnessed one candidate include one-armed push-ups in her solo audition routine. Then she threw one leg over the arm and continued to do one-armed, one-legged push-ups. The judges and spectators were awestruck and she received applause for her feat. But she did not make the cut. Arena cheerleading is a dance style, not an aerobics competition. I can almost guarantee no NFL, NBA or other pro dance team will ever include one-armed, one-legged push-ups in a routine!

- **Tap**. Tap dance is fun, but the movements are vastly different from what you will do on the field or on the court. Tap dance has its own vocabulary of movement, and very few moves will translate to your arena cheerleading routines. However, it can be a great way to build stamina, strength, and memorization of choreography skills.

- **Yoga**. This is a great style for increasing flexibility, stamina, and general fitness. However, you will not learn any of the turns, leaps, or dance positions that you will need to be fluent in before auditioning for a pro dance squad. Yoga also uses the flexed foot position in most moves, so you will not get to develop the strength of your toe-point. If you are an expert yogi, you will still need to take some other form of dance to adequately prepare for your audition.

- **Hula**. Hawaiian hula dance has some benefits because it will loosen hips, make your hands graceful, and work on toning your stomach, but the arm movements are very soft and you will not learn the technical moves that you will need to know.

- **Irish step dance**. This is probably the best form of dance for working on high, quick kicks with pointed toes. Most pro dance teams have at least one kick-line routine, so having great kicks is an asset. However, this style focuses on a still torso and serious expression, and does not do enough to develop your arm movement to its full potential. While it is great to develop your kicks in this class, you should still seek another dance class to work on technique and overall style.

- **Burlesque**. Burlesque is one of the newest dance fitness class styles on the scene. It is a fun, flirty, performance-based dance style modeled after the old-world burlesque shows. The attire usually incorporates lacy two-piece sets, feather boas, high heels, and other flirty accessories. Many gyms and dance studios are offering this dance style alongside the more traditional classes. I highly recommend taking a burlesque class for the fun of it, and it will help you develop your showmanship and stage personality. However, there is usually very little emphasis on technical dance steps such as turns, so this class alone will not adequately prepare you for an arena cheer audition.

- **The Electric Slide and the Macarena.** Okay, I put these two in here just to see if you are paying attention! It goes without saying that neither of these will prepare you for a rigorous audition routine. But they might help loosen you up and make you smile if you do them in your head the morning before the audition starts!

As a general pointer, no matter which style you do, remember to practice smiling while you dance. Whenever you have a performance opportunity, even if it is half the class dancing for the other half during a weekly class, use that chance to work on your smile and performance skills. Face control while dancing is an often forgotten element for many dancers. Be aware of what your face is doing, and then learn to control it just like you would control your arms or legs.

Lastly, I recommend that you tell your dance teacher you plan to audition for a pro cheer squad. Ask for as much feedback and critique as possible. That way, he or she will help guide your development to meet your goals. And you never know, maybe your teacher knows someone who knows someone who knows someone who can help you make the team! It is a very small world, after all.

Should you take gymnastics?

If you do not have an existing gymnastics background, it is probably not good use of your time to start learning as an adult. The process is long and the risk of injury is high. Unlike dance, which can be learned late in life, gymnastics seems to take longer to process for adult learners. If you are going to take lessons, focus on dance instead. Very few arena cheer squads require gymnastics, but all of them require dance!

What to do about flexibility issues

Many teams require that their dancers perform high kicks and splits. Your low kick could keep you off the team! Your goal should be to have splits on both sides (left and right) and high kicks that can practically touch your nose (but please don't kick your nose!).

If you cannot do the splits or if your kicks are low, you will need to work on your flexibility early. Flexibility is developed over time, and rushing the process will result in injury that could set you back or prevent you from auditioning. So take it slowly!

Yoga, classical ballet, hybrid ballet barre fitness classes, gymnastics, and specialty stretching classes are good choices for developing flexibility. With time and effort, almost anyone can achieve greater levels of flexibility.

How pom-poms can sabotage your routine

Most dance classes do not include the use of pom-poms, unless you are lucky enough to find an arena cheerleading dance class in your city.

So while a good jazz class will certainly teach you the leaps, turns, kicks, and arm positions you need to be a great dancer, you will likely not have the opportunity to practice these moves while holding pom-poms.

Most professional cheerleaders that dance for football teams use pom-poms in their routines. For professional basketball and other sports, the use of pom-poms varies.

Part of your research involved determining whether your dream team uses pom-poms, and if so, whether pom-poms will be used at the auditions. If so, then you will want to practice dancing with pom-poms in your hands at least part of the time so that you are used to how it feels to move with pom-poms.

The poms add weight to your arms, especially the larger poms, making it harder to hit moves sharply. You must also hold the pom-poms correctly so that your hand does not cock into a funny position when you hit each arm position.

If you have no or little experience dancing with pom-poms, you should practice doing so as soon as possible. Many audition candidates have been caught off guard when handed a pair of pom-poms to dance with. You don't want your first time dancing with pom-poms in your hands to be in front of judges!

Practicing ahead of time will have you swinging the poms like a pro. As an added benefit, the poms will add weight to your hands when you rehearse, giving you a great workout! It is also a lot of fun to dance with poms, since you will be able to visualize yourself out on the field or court easier when you see yourself in your mirror with pom-poms in each hand.

If you need to purchase pom-poms, simply click here to go to Amazon.com to order some. The best kind have a baton or dowel handle (where the handle is a wooden or plastic bar, with pom-pom streamers coming out both ends) and 3/4" to 1" wide streamers. The best streamer length is anywhere from 6" to 10." You can also go to **eBay.com** or **craigslist.com** to see if anyone is selling used poms.

Seek experienced teachers

Did you know that many professional cheerleaders (or former cheerleaders) teach dance at local studios full time or as a side job? Or that many might be willing to give private lessons if asked? Do some research to see if this is the case by asking the team director, reading the cheerleader bio pages, and asking studios if any of their teachers have that background. A current or alumni pro cheerleader would make a great coach and mentor, and would likely be worth the expense.

Also see if your local pro teams offer workshops or audition prep bootcamps. These are a great way to learn about the team, meet the director, and see which dance style the team uses! These may not be well advertised, so this is another reason to research your team carefully, join all of its mailing lists and social networking fan pages, and contact the team director.

If group classes are not available near you, consider asking a current or alumni pro cheerleader to give you private lessons.

Arena Cheerleader Bootcamp & Retreat

After years of coaching and mentoring audition candidates one-on-one, and in conjunction with developing an Arena Cheerleading dance course I teach at a local college, I am offering interested women the chance to attend a LIVE Arena Cheerleader Bootcamp & Retreat.

This is not for everyone, but if you are interested in learning from the nation's top choreographers and getting personalized feedback about your look, dance ability, and interview skills, then please consider working with me at a future Arena Cheerleader Bootcamp & Retreat.

Please join the **www.ArenaCheerleader.com** mailing list to be notified when registration for the next event is available. Mailing list members are the first to hear about early bird specials and discounts!

Arena Cheerleader Bootcamp & Retreat details:

- Multi-day LIVE event held in a beautiful location

- Special workshops for aspiring pro cheerleaders, current pro cheerleaders, alumni pro cheerleaders, and dance team directors

- Aspiring pro cheerleaders are paired with mentors for one-on-one personal coaching

- All attendees learn exciting arena-style routines taught by some of the industry's top choreographers

- All attendees receive a pair of pom-poms and matching dancewear

- Any attendee may participate in an "as-close-to-real-as-we-can-make-it" mock audition, judged by an experienced panel of actual pro-level judges, where each candidate receives her score evaluation sheets with the judges' feedback and comments

- Expert speakers will present on health, fitness, media skills, interview techniques, leadership, makeup, hair, and motivation

- Sponsors and vendors will give attendees exciting goodies, giveaways, samples, and discounts

- (OPTIONAL) Early-bird registrants may register for the optional photocard photo shoot or swimsuit calendar photo shoot, both shot by well-known professional sports photographers

- All attendees will receive a bootcamp graduation diploma stating completion of the training, which may be used later on audition applications and resumes

- Attendees get to network with each other and make lifelong friends!

- **Limited seats available at each event and each retreat will likely sell out; register early!**

Join the **www.ArenaCheerleader.com** mailing list to be notified when registration opens.

Hope to see you there!

Other great audition bootcamps

I know of many other fantastic bootcamp and audition preparation workshops offered nationwide, so if the Arena Cheerleader Bootcamp & Retreat described above is not the right fit for you, if registration is full, or if you want to attend more than one retreat, please consider some of the other phenomenal training camps out there.

Do some research to see what might be available in your region.

Here's a great resource started up by Laura (Eilers) Clark, who cheered for the St. Louis Rams, Kansas City Chiefs, and Kansas City Wizards. She was crowned Ms. Virginia United States and then received the national crown as the 2011 Ms. United States. She now directs two state Miss United States pageants for District of Columbia and Delaware in addition to owning Going Pro Entertainment.

Going Pro Entertainment is a network of pro cheer alumni who offer choreography expos, team training, and private audition coaching. They have representatives in nearly every major U.S. market and Canada. Take a look at **www.goingproentertainment.com** to see what is offered near you! Laura is a fabulous resource and her organization is top-notch.

Another phenomenal training resource is Sideline Ready. It was founded by Sabrina Ellison, who has been actively involved in the professional dance and cheerleading world for almost two decades. Having danced in the NFL for 8 seasons and as the current NBA Dance Team Director for the Golden State Warriors, she recognized a huge void in performance training for aspiring professional performers. She created Sideline Ready to help fill that void.

Sideline Ready is a collaboration of professional dance team directors, pro dancers, cheerleaders, and sports entertainment producers that know exactly what it takes to cultivate and mentor raw talent to be Sideline Ready. The program has guided many professional performers both domestically and internationally on gaining the confidence, look and standout performance quality necessary to become a professional cheerleader. The website is **www.sidelineready.com**.

I will help promote all of these bootcamp events to my mailing list, so be sure you have visited **www.ArenaCheerleader.com** to join it so that you are the first to hear about new training opportunities.

When should you choreograph your own dance?

Many arena cheerleader candidates are taken by surprise when they realize they need to perform a solo self-choreographed routine as part of the audition process. Not all teams require this, and for the ones that do, this portion is usually only for finalists rather than during the earlier rounds of cuts.

Review the audition information carefully to see if a self-choreographed routine is required, and whether there are any length requirements (for example, a six 8-count maximum length). Some teams will allow you to wear a different outfit for the solo, while others require that you wear the same clothing as for your group audition. Sometimes the details are only revealed to the finalists at the end of the preliminary rounds. That's why it is a good idea to prepare a routine ahead of time, so that you have a head start.

I recommend choreographing a routine at least four weeks prior to the audition, but preferably two to three months before for maximum confidence and peace of mind. It is very stressful to perform your solo, and needing to concentrate on unrehearsed choreography will add to your nervousness.

The idea is to perform your solo routine as polished and confidently as possible. It needs to look like a final product that you could perform on a stage, not something you hastily put together for the audition.

You should choose a style that shows off your talents, but keep in mind you should stick to styles that mesh with arena cheerleader dance. Please refer to the section in this book on dance styles for help selecting a dance form. A safe bet is to include at least one technical skill (like a double-turn pirouette), at least one high kick to show your flexibility, at least one move with hair flipping or other hair action to add drama, and at least one or two 8-counts of dance moves with intense hip and torso action to add excitement and fun to the routine.

One way to put together a great solo routine is to take individual 8-counts from routines you have learned in dance classes or on other dance teams to create your own hybrid routine. Choose 8-counts that you find fun to perform, that are already part of your muscle memory, and that you can perform particularly well.

Also, sometimes the audition choreography that you will be taught at auditions will include some "freestyle" 8-counts at the beginning of the routine. In addition to choreographing your own solo routine, you should also have an 8-count ready that you can use when asked to add some freestyle during the introductory beats of the choreographed dance. It can include some step-clapping with some arm pumps or graceful arm swings, or perhaps some sassy turns—always with a smile, of course!

Be sure to rehearse your routines with your hair down, and really learn to use your hair as part of your body, like an arm. You can learn to flip your hair with the same precision you use to position an arm!

Polish each step of your solo so that you can perform it automatically without concentrating on choreography. This will allow you to focus on what it is truly important—connecting with the judges!

Occasionally, I will send sample choreography videos to the **www.ArenaCheerleader.com** mailing list. Join the list today to get in on those emailed videos! Some videos will also be posted to the Arena Cheerleader™ Facebook® page at **www.facebook.com/ArenaCheerleader**, so be sure to visit and hit "**LIKE**" today!

Chapter 5:
Your Body

What is the ideal body you need to sculpt?

In the myth-busting section, I explained that cheerleading is for fit, athletic women, not skinny undernourished waifs. This is a power sport, and to be powerful you need some muscles and lots of energy!

The worst thing you can do for your body is to starve yourself or to go on a fad diet to prepare for auditions. The tips below will help you achieve the right body type appropriate for the demands of this sport.

Fitness level required

To be able to dance for many hours in a row, with a high level of enthusiasm from start to finish, you will need energy. That means that you have to be fit and athletic. Take an honest look at your body and fitness routine. Is there anything you can do to increase your fitness level? Do you exercise regularly enough? Do you get winded climbing stairs? Can you jog 50 yards and come out on the other side smiling, the way you might on a football field? Or does your energy peter out after being active for 15 minutes?

If you cannot maintain high energy for hours at a time, then you will need to work on your stamina. The best way to do this is by taking dance classes, running, participating in active hobbies like skiing and horse riding, and making a habit of choosing the parking spot FURTHEST from the entrance (yes, no more roaming the parking lot for the closest space!).

Take the stairs at work rather than the elevator. Move a little faster when vacuuming your rugs. Take morning or evening speed-walks as a way to meet up with friends rather than sitting around together. Swim more. Walk away from your desk every hour or so at work to do some sort of brief cardio, even if it is taking the stairs one floor up to the other floor's water cooler rather than using the one on your own floor.

Make small lifestyle changes like these to increase your overall stamina. This will help you on the day of auditions as well, once you are on the team. What are the lifestyle changes you will commit to make? Write them down and get started!

Looking athletic

Besides increasing your energy and stamina, you will need to exercise so that you look toned and athletic. The two will go hand-in-hand, because a fit person looks athletic and also has more energy.

When you see six-pack abs and rock-hard arm muscles on a dancer, it is evidence of hard work and a great fitness routine. Almost any form of exercise, when done regularly, will tone your body and give you a fit look. The best are dancing, martial arts, kickboxing, volleyball, basketball, mountain biking, skiing, snowboarding, yoga, and other forms of exercise that combine a variety of motion, strength training, and high-intensity cardio.

The more cross-training you do among sports, the more overall fitness you will achieve. And your body will reflect the evidence of your efforts! What will you add to your repertoire?

Muscles

Many women fear developing bulky muscles and don't incorporate weight-lifting into their fitness routine due to that fear. But the truth is that nothing will sculpt your body faster than a workout plan that includes working your muscles. Having greater muscle mass will help increase your overall metabolism and will get you those abs and arms you want to show off at auditions.

Personal trainers are recommended, because it is dangerous to lift weights using improper technique. You want to have someone monitor your progress and correct your posture to ensure you are doing things correctly.

If a personal trainer is outside of your budget, consider finding a group fitness training class near you. Group training can offer you the supervision and encouragement you would get from a personal trainer, but with a lower cost since the trainer has other students in the same class with you.

One great group training franchise is Crossfit®. See if they offer group weight training near you at **www.crossfit.com**. You might be able to work out a deal at a local Crossfit gym if you tell the owner your goals and offer to give a client testimonial if and when you make it onto the arena dance team of your dreams.

Nutrition

You need to fuel your body correctly in order to develop the lean, strong, toned look that will get you high marks at auditions.

Many books have been written on dieting, so I won't reinvent the wheel here. You have probably tried one or more diets in your life, especially when one diet comes into the spotlight due to celebrity endorsement or great marketing. So which is best for the cheerleader body? Low fat? No fat? Low carb? No carb? Vegetarian? Vegan? Carnivore? South Beach®? Atkins®? The Virgin Diet®? Eating like a cavewoman on the Paleo diet? The list of diets out there is endless. So is the nutrition bookshelf in the book store.

Everybody is different, and every body will respond to a diet differently. The only way to discover the best diet for you is to try different ways of eating until you find the way that gives you energy while allowing you to meet your weight-loss or weight-maintenance goals.

Fad diets rarely having any lasting effects. If it sounds too good to be true, it probably is. If it sounds too extreme, stay away. This means you should avoid the diet where you eat and buy only special chocolate chip cookies, or the one where you only eat cabbage soup for a week. Any extreme diet where you eat only one food, such as a fruit juice cleanse, should be used as an occasional detox only, and always under the supervision of a doctor.

In general, the best diets are the ones that cut out processed foods, fried foods, refined sugar, high fructose corn syrup, alcohol, and empty calorie starches. Basically, if it has a shelf life, it's probably overly processed and should be replaced with its fresh equivalent. This means you should choose fresh fruit over canned, fresh chicken over frozen fried chicken fingers, and water over soda or alcohol. If you cut the processed junk out of your diet, you will be left eating relatively healthy foods.

My favorite diets to recommend are:

- **The Paleo Diet.** The Paleo diet is based on the belief that our stomachs and digestive system developed around the time of Paleolithic man, and never evolved beyond that despite the changes in how we feed our bodies. Under the Paleo diet theory, we do not digest mass-produced grains and other processed foods properly because those foods did not exist at the time our stomachs stopped evolving. I know many people who have found success following the principles behind this plan, which include sticking to a diet containing mostly lean protein, lots of vegetables, nuts, and some fruits. There are some great books written about this diet, including *Practical Paleo, The Paleo Solution,* and *The Paleo Diet.*

- **The Virgin Diet.** Author J.J. Virgin wrote a book about a simple plan that cuts out all of the foods that cause the most inflammation in her patients. You do this for a three-week period, with a gradual testing timeline during which each food is reintroduced to discover the foods that you should avoid. She explains how most people have allergic or inflammatory responses to seven trigger foods like soy, gluten, sugar, peanuts, dairy, eggs, and corn. This is a good plan to try if you think you might have a food sensitivity but are not sure which one. Get her book, *The Virgin Diet,* to learn more.

- **The South Beach Diet.** This classic diet promotes eating a balanced meal comprised of the right percentage of carbohydrates versus protein versus fats versus dairy. Many have found great success with these principles, and I know many people who have personally found this is an easy plan to stick to once learned. The book is available at *The South Beach Diet Supercharged.*

- **The Zone Diet.** Massachusetts Institute of Technology researcher Dr. Barry Sears created the Zone Diet, based on Nobel Prize-winning research. His book contains lists of good and bad carbohydrates and easy-to-follow food blocks.

- **The Crazy Sexy Diet.** Kris Carr survived cancer and is now an outspoken advocate for cleaner living. Her diet plan cuts out processed and toxin-rich foods to live a cleaner life. The best part is—the diet is not only good for your overall health, but also helps you achieve a slim and sexy figure. Get her book, Crazy Sexy Diet, on Amazon.

- **The Slow Carb Diet**. Tim Ferris is the creator of this diet. On it, you eat the right kind of carbs daily, paired with one "binge" day per week when you can eat anything you want for a 24-hour period. It is a balance between discipline for six days with utter gluttony on the seventh day. He describes how to automate your breakfast choices and maximize fat burning. Check out his book, the *4-Hour Body.*

Keep in mind that the diets above are all different from each other, just like your body is different from mine or anybody else's. The diet that will work best for you is the one that makes you feel the best. When you are eating correctly, you should have lots of energy and should be slim and strong.

For some women, a vegan diet will work best. For another, the Paleo diet is the way to go. And the best diet for each of us can also change over time, so that what you should eat at age 25 might evolve into a different optimum nutrition plan at age 35.

If you are not feeling energetic or are carrying around a lot of extra weight, please consult your doctor and then experiment with healthy eating plans until you find the one that works for you. It should be one that contains nutritious foods and that you can maintain for the long term.

Does this make you feel overwhelmed? If the thought of diets and food plans distresses you and you know you can't make a big commitment, then start small. Sometimes when something seems too big to accomplish, like changing our entire eating habits, it's easier to keep our heads in the sand and not even try.

That avoidance behavior isn't helping anyone, so here's an idea to get you started:

Before making any major changes, why don't you start with changing just one meal? I recommend starting with breakfast. Breakfast is the easiest meal of the day to automate, because you generally are home in the morning. Lunch and dinner can be tougher nuts to crack because you are on-the-go more often for those meals, or out with friends, but breakfast is usually in a controlled setting.

If you always begin your day with a balanced breakfast that includes lean protein, fruits high in antioxidants, healthy fats and whole grains or non-starchy vegetables, then the rest of the day will be easier to conquer.

If you are interested in learning how to make that switch in an easy way, check out the Special Report & Recipe Guide you can download for free from the **ArenaCheerleader.com** website. It's called "What should a professional cheerleader eat for breakfast? And it's NOT Cheerios®!" and you get a free copy of it when you join the Arena Cheerleader mailing list.

I co-authored it with nutrition expert Grace Suh, who is a fantastic resource for nutrition coaching. It had to be cut out of this book due to size, but it is worth the read and I hope you make the breakfast switch. Download the report and recipes, tape it to your pantry door, and see how great you feel when you do breakfast right every day!

Hydration

Very few of us are drinking enough water. In addition, the typical American diet is full of processed foods and fast food that can contain a lot of salt. Excess salt causes your body to hoard water, resulting in water retention and puffiness.

Besides making us puffy, hydration issues can also cause a lack of energy and make you feel tired. By not drinking enough liquids, your body won't recover from workouts as quickly and you will not perform as well athletically.

You should make it a point to drink at least three to five liters of water per day. Yes, LITERS, not glasses! That may sound like a lot, but once you reach that level and maintain it for a few weeks, you will see your energy level soar. You will also see improvement in your skin tone, physical performance, mental acuity, and endurance. If that's not enough motivation, how about the fact that many women see a reduction in the appearance of cellulite once their body stops retaining water? Drink up!

Make it a point to begin and end each day with at least one liter of water upon waking and before bed. This will get you almost halfway to your daily intake. Then develop a habit of carrying a water bottle with you wherever you go.

Finally, when at work or at your desk, set a timer so that you take a water and brisk walk break at least once every hour. This will help you with hydration as well as fatigue from your workday routine.

When dancing, it is especially important that you maintain proper hydration. Before and after a dance class, be sure to replenish your body's fluids. Skip the sugary sports drinks—especially the ones with artificial sweeteners—and opt for nature's tried and true sports drink instead: pure water!

Energy

When we want extra energy, many of us turn to caffeine, sugar, or packaged energy products like 5-Hour Energy®. The danger with this type of manufactured energy is that it can lead to crashes, insulin spikes, and addiction.

One of your goals in maintaining an optimal fitness, nutrition, and hydration regimen is to find a natural way to have sustained energy throughout the day. If you follow the advice in this book with respect to working out and eating right, and drink lots of purified water, you will probably be able to stop relying on artificial energy sources.

You will find your body's natural state is an energetic one, and this natural lasting energy will help you look and feel your best on the day of auditions. If you must have some caffeine in your system, try switching to green tea or yerba maté, both rich in antioxidants.

Remember, in many ways cheerleaders are the embodiment of pure energy into the physical form, from the fan's perspective. Everything about you should project energy. If you work hard at your nutrition, hydration, and fitness, the right level of energy will be the natural result.

Chapter 6:

Your Grooming

What is the ideal "look" you need to create?

This section addresses grooming and appearance, so that you can develop the right look that judges will score highly on the day of tryouts. Of course, the nutrition, exercise and hydration chapter of this book also help you with your look, because your physical fitness level obviously contributes to your appearance.

But here, we will go beyond your body's natural fitness level to explore the concepts of makeup, hair, and accessories. Later in this book, I will also explain how to dress, but for this chapter, we will focus on the non-apparel aspects of your ideal look.

Your goal is to transform your looks to align with the way the team of your dreams styles its members. The team director wants cheerleaders who are unique, but who can fit in with the overall image of the team.

Even though uniqueness is a plus, at the auditions you should focus on fitting in, not standing out. I don't mean that you should be unremarkable and forgettable; of course not! You do need to stand out, but you should stand out for your superior dance ability and excellent grooming, not because you present yourself in a completely different way than the other applicants. The director does not want a dancer who will stand out in a negative way. If you stand out, make yourself stand out by being an even better fit than existing team members.

Part of your research was to determine what that look is for each team that you are interested in cheering for. Keep those specific variations in mind when reading the general information in this chapter.

How do you stand out while blending in? This is a complicated concept, I know. The answer is that you should groom yourself the way that the existing team members groom themselves. This means makeup, hair, and accessories should blend in with the team's current look. Any body type and face type can be made to fit that "look."

Then your own natural features, energy, smile, and dance ability will be the factors that "stand out" while your grooming and accessories "blend in." This is the balance you need to find between standing out while blending in.

When designing your makeup and hair, take a look at the team's current photocard. The team director most likely hired a hair stylist and makeup artist to help each dancer achieve the right look. Keep that in mind.

The section below will analyze each type of appearance element separately with individual comments for each that you should take into account.

Hair is a part of your body for dance moves

Your hair can make or break it for you. Soft, full hair that moves with you when you dance is as important to your dancing as your arm and body placement. Almost all arena dance routines will include a hair toss move (or two or three or four or more!) and most teams require their cheerleaders to dance with their hair completely down.

Your hair color should be complementary to your skin tone. If your hair color is not fit to grace the cover of a box of at-home color product, then it is not the right color for your tryout. For example, if you have harsh platinum highlights against deep black hair, this is an extreme look that you won't see on a box of Clairol® at your local drugstore.

Color:

My recommendations for color are simple:

- **Color**. Pick a glossy color that is in style. Look at the team's photocard and select a color that would fit in with the team. It is easiest to match the color with someone already on the team. Remember, the team director approved every hair color currently on the team. In general, if you don't see the color in ads for hair color, it's not in style. You can visit hair color manufacturer websites to see the colors they have available. You can also ask your stylist to show you the color swatch books. The biggest mistake I see is when brunettes choose a burgundy, almost purple color that is too deep and inky for their skin tone. I also often see strawberry-blonde and red done with amateur-looking color. Blonde hair can look amazing, but also terrible when the hair looks fried or over-processed. Unsightly grown-out roots are also a common issue. If you are gong to go with blonde or any of the red or strawberry-blonde tones, you should really go to a professional to make sure it is done correctly. Brown tones are the easiest to do at home, but can look flat if you do not use a product that has natural lowlights and highlights built in. Lastly, most women can't go wrong with their natural hair color, so when in doubt, stick to what you were born with!

- **Highlights.** I advise against high-contrast highlights because of how often I see them backfire. Harsh highlights can make someone look older, and it is important to keep the highlights and lowlights close enough in shade that you don't end up with streaked "skunk" hair. If you have an excellent stylist and have people in the pro cheer industry to give you personal honest feedback, go for it. But beware the pitfalls of at-home highlight kits or stylists who end up making you look modern and hip, but too far off the charts to fit in with the dance team's look. Consider whether you see a lot of team members with highlights, and how subtle or defined they are when deciding if you should go down that path.

- **Shine.** Dry, fried hair does not audition well. You need to make sure your choice of color does not dry your hair out. Platinum blondes can look especially harsh and "beat" when they have straw-like dry hair. No matter what you do with color, highlights, or products, your goal should be to maintain glossy healthy-looking hair. Keep that in mind. If you are blonde, be sure you are a healthy-looking blonde, not a frizzy damaged-hair blonde.

Cut & Length:

The best cuts are those with some layering at the bottom to give the hair movement. The goal is to have hair that stays off of your face when you hit a dance pose, yet moves easily with you during each dance move. Ideally, you want something you can toss! If your head whips up, your hair should add flair and drama to that dance move.

Avoid bangs if you have a choice. Fringe or solid across-the-whole-forehead bangs will not stay in place during heavy dancing. They will also stick to your forehead if you get sweaty. If you must have bangs, side-sweep bangs move the best for dancing, but be sure to rehearse dancing with your bangs for at least a few weeks before the audition. New bangs usually end up in a dancer's eyes when she has no experience moving her head the right way during dance moves to keep her hair out of her face.

Longer hair, so long as it is healthy looking, works best for auditions. Avoid cutting your hair too short before auditions. Shoulder-length or longer is best. Pixie-cuts and other shorter hairstyles don't leave your team director with many choices about your look once you make the team. If all cheerleaders on the team have longer hair, take that as a sign that you should let yours grow out as long as possible before auditions. However, don't sacrifice healthy hair for length. If your ends are fried and dry, you will need to get regular trims so that the ends of your hair look great on the day of auditions.

In general, you will see more NBA dancers with short hair than you will find in the NFL. But it is still not a common hairstyle in pro cheerleading, so longer hair is your goal. The optimal length is at your bra strap, or an inch or two above or below it. It is risky to have your hair longer than that, because ultra-long hair can look heavy, make you look unbalanced, and not move correctly during dancing. There was a dancer at one audition with hair that was longer than her waist. It got tangled around her as she danced because it was so long. Unfortunately, that is all I remember about her. You want to be remembered for YOU, not for your hair!

If you have shorter, thin hair and you know that you would look fantastic with longer, thicker hair, consider getting hair extensions. These can add instant length and thickness. The extensions will add fullness, but at a hefty cost if done right. Don't get bargain-store extensions! They should look absolutely natural, or don't get them at all. If you have the time and money to invest in extensions, give it a try long enough before auditions that you will be able to rehearse with them to adjust to the added weight.

You need a cut that you do not need to constantly adjust. When you are on the floor, you should not touch or adjust your hair at all when in front of the judges. You should not sweep your bangs to the side with your hand, you should not brush you hair off your shoulders, and you should not fluff it up manually. In other words, no primping in front of the judges! This means you need a cut that will not require constant adjustment. You should be able to dance with it and have it fall naturally into place at the end of your dance routine.

Style:

Which of the current team members has a hairstyle that would look great on your own features? Use that as a guide and ask your stylist how you can make the best out of your hair cut by styling it correctly. Hair stylists are usually more than happy to show you how to use hot rollers, curling irons, and other styling products if you are a regular client. You can even make an appointment the morning of auditions to have the pro handle your styling for you!

Another way to find great looks is to analyze the hairstyles worn on local and national news programs by the younger female anchors and weather reporters. The stylists on news shows generally stick to loose hair with a polished look for the women aged in their 20's and early 30's, and most of these looks would work well at a professional cheerleading audition.

If you do not know whether to go straight, curly, or wavy... if you are feeling lost and overwhelmed and your stylist keeps trying to get you to try something you know won't work, then here's an easy default hair style you can wear on the day of auditions, if your hair type responds well to heat and curlers:

- **Wash**. Wash and condition your hair with a sulfate-free shampoo and conditioner. Why sulfate-free? Sulfates can dry your hair and reduce shine, and can also strip away color.

- **Towel-dry**. Towel-dry your hair to get out much of the moisture.

- **Leave-in conditioner.** Comb or brush it out when you get out of the shower with a dab of a leave-in conditioner like Sebastian Potion 9® (this is my go-to when straightening curly hair) or leave-in oil like MorroccanOil®(this whole line of products is fantastic and smells like heaven!). Use the leave-in only on the section from your ears down (i.e. stay away form your hairline or the top of your head, since we don't want that area oily or weighed down).

- **Styling product**. Use a large dab of alcohol-free hair gel or styling spray and spread evenly through all of your hair (anything that will add hold without stiffness). My favorite brand is Dep® Sport, which is alcohol-free and very inexpensive. Add a spritz of hairspray or thickening spray just on the roots of your hair. You can do this by parting your hair in several different places and lightly spritzing your scalp at each part before parting your hair in a new spot. Comb your hair to make sure the styling product is well-distributed.

- **Dry**. Using a large round brush, blow-dry your hair in sections while using the brush to smooth each strand as you dry it. Any hairdryer is fine, but many women find that ones with ionic technology and ceramic keep their hair shinier. Pull outwards, not downwards. Dry the roots especially well, and do so while holding the hair up so that you get lift at the crown of your head.

- **Velcro® curlers**. Using Velcro® curlers that are 2" to 3" in size, take sections of hair and roll each section onto a curler, securing with a clip (be sure the clip placement does not create a kink in your hair!). The ones on the top of your head should be rolled up and back, while the sides of your head should be rolled out and down.

- **Set**. Using the hottest yet lowest speed setting on your hairdryer, continue to dry the hair while it is in curlers. You can also use a dryer bonnet. Your goal is to have it be bone-dry before you unroll the curlers.

- **Spray**. Take the hair out of the rollers, and before brushing or doing anything with each strand, mist an aerosol hair spray over your entire head lightly. Let the spray air-dry.

- **Brush out**. Next, brush out the curls with either your fingers, or a wide-toothed comb. The idea is to have natural, body-filled waves and soft, loose curls. There should be a lot of lift at your roots, because the curlers caused the hair to dry with the roots of the strands perpendicular to your scalp. If you have fine hair, you can also tease your hair at the crown for even greater lift and body.

- **Shine**. Spritz a small amount of shine-enhancing spray over your hair, avoiding the roots and top of your head. The best one I have found is by BioSilk®, but any lightweight shine spray will work.

That's it! Two tips: Don't show up at registration in curlers. This is not the best impression to make! And second, take a large-barreled curling iron and all of your products to the audition for touch-ups. Third, you should wear your hair the same way for both the dance portion and interview portions, so that there's no confusion as to who you are and to build a link between your dance and interview identities. Now, flip that hair and dance, dance, dance!

Makeup

To find a great makeup look for yourself, carefully analyze the individual team member photos that you can find online. Most arena dance teams will post biographies and individual photos of team members. If this is not available, then look at the team photo, which will not show as much detail but will still give you a good sampling of dancer makeup looks.

Which of the current team members has on makeup that would look great on your own features? Use that as a guide. Take that photo to a local makeup sales counter. I recommend a M.A.C Cosmetics® counter if your local mall has one because that brand specializes in the entertainment industry. Another option is to find a Sephora® store to experiment on yourself with all of their sample colors and products. You can ask a salesperson at any makeup counter if you can have a makeover lesson, using the dance team photo as a guide for the makeup artist. Tell him or her that you want to learn how to create the look worn by the dance team member.

Another way to find great looks is to analyze the makeup worn on local and national news programs by the younger female anchors and weather reporters, just like you did for finding hairstyles. The makeup artists on news shows generally stick to a professional yet bold makeup look for the women anchors who are in their 20's and early 30's. These are good looks to emulate.

When you try a new look, take a photo of yourself to see how that makeup style will look to others and in photos. A camera is more reliable than a mirror, and lets you save looks you have created for future reference and reproduction.

Here is a general guideline for creating a great professional cheerleader makeup look:

- **Moisturizer**. Begin by making sure you have enough moisturizer on your face. You do not want to have dry skin cause your foundation to get flaky or for it to settle into fine lines caused by dry skin. Begin your makeup ritual by testing your skin for dryness, and lightly massaging in a small amount of extra moisturizer before you begin applying foundation.

- **Concealer**. Use concealer for dark circles, in the inner corners of your eyes, at the outer corners of your lips, along the crease from nostrils to the corners of your lips, along the sides of your nostrils, at the outer corners of both eyes, and on any scars, moles, pimples, and red marks. Using a small brush similar to a paintbrush works best for dabbing and stroking concealer into place.

- **Foundation**. Choose a foundation with extra coverage for dance auditions. You do not want sheer or light coverage; this is the time to bring out the big guns! The idea is to create a flawless finish, like they wear on television. Your M.A.C Cosmetics® counter will have foundation formulas with this type of heavy coverage. Just be sure the color goes with your face and also matches your body. There's nothing odder than seeing a face that looks like it was morphed onto a different body with Photoshop® because the skin tones are so different! Again, use a brush or sponge to dab and stroke the foundation into a satin-smooth coverage over your entire face, including your neckline. Watch out for the areas by your ears, eyebrows, and hairline, since these must be done carefully to avoid a line or accidentally applying makeup to your hair. Many women apply foundation over their brows, and then wipe off the excess from the hair surface. Others carefully edge around eyebrows—either technique is fine to use.

- **Powder**. Finish off your foundation with a light dusting of a matching powder. You will use this powder throughout the day to combat shine when you get sweaty from dancing.

- **Brows**. Use a brow powder or pencil to define your brows. My favorite powder is Anastasia® for women with naturally-thin eyebrows, but I also really like Brow Zings by Benefit® because it contains a wax as well as a powder to tame thicker or unruly brows. And you have to love the fact that it contains a tiny pair of tweezers in the compact!

- **Eyeshadow.** Your eyeshadow should consist of at least three shades of color. One is a light shimmery color to use just under your eyebrows, another is a medium tone color to use along the crease and on the lid, and the third is a very dark deep color to use exclusively in the crease and along your lid line over your eyeliner. The third color can also be used over eyeliner under your eyes if you choose to create a smoky look.

  + **Light shimmery color:** Any light shimmer will work, and I recommend neutrals or barely-there colors like bone, gold, silver, opalescent, light grey, or pearl. The "shimmer" is optional, because a matte non-shimmer color works fine as long as is it a very light color. Examples are Nylon by M.A.C Cosmetics® and the All Over Shimmer Duo by Stila®. This is the first color you add, and it goes just under your eyebrows along your browbone and in the inner corners of your eyes.

  + **Medium tone for crease and lids:** This is your main color. If you want to add punch, this is where you showcase your color of choice (stick with neutrals for the light and deep tones, but feel free to experiment with color here for the medium tone). Try a purple, green or blue if you have brown eyes, grey or plum for blue eyes, and emerald or royal for green eyes. If you have already selected an audition outfit, see which shade works best with the color of your top. Do not try to incorporate more than one color here; stick with one main color to avoid eyes that look too busy. This color gets applied all over your lids and into the crease. You can find eyeshadow palettes that have many different colors to let you experiment with different beautiful shades, like the Shades of Nature Eye Shadow Palette by Sephora®.

  + **Deep tone for crease and over eyeliner:** Choose a dark, matte color to be used in the crease of your eye. This is the shade that will give your eyes drama. If you decide to go for a smoky look, this is the shade you will also apply over your eyeliner along your lash lines above and below your eyes. Try deep smoke, deepest brown, dark purple, or even black. Use this sparingly to avoid looking like you have two black eyes! And after applying, use a soft fluffy brush to blend the edges well so that this color looks blended in rather than painted on.

- **Eyeliner**. The idea behind your audition makeup is to make your face stand out. Even if you normally don't use eyeliner, you should use it at auditions so that your eyes do not blend in to your face under the bright lights. Stick with matte neutrals like brown, black, and dark grey. If you are a beginner, I recommend using an eyeliner that you draw on with a pen-like felt-tip applicator, which is a lot easier to use than the type you have to paint on with a small flexible bristle brush. You have less control with the bristles, since the hairs on the brush head can separate as you add pressure, making your line uneven in width. The felt-tip pens give you more control. My favorite is the Artliner by Lancome®. If you have small eyes, one option is to apply a white or light pink liner to your lash lines just inside of where you apply the dark liner, but be careful not to get any liner in your eyes because this could irritate them.

- **Sparkle**. For added pizzazz, use a glitter or sparkle element very sparingly to accent your face. Do not go overboard with sparkle, but a touch of it can give you a glamorous punch that will help you shine out on the dance floor! You can dab some sparkle gold or silver to the inside corner of each eye, or to the outside corner if that works better for your face shape. Try both and see which you prefer. Another place to add a touch of colorless sparkle is along the top of your cheekbones.

- **False lashes**. Before putting on mascara, consider applying false lashes to your eyes for an ultra-glamorous and show-time-worthy look. These are not easy to apply, so be sure to practice gluing them on often before committing to using them on the day of audition. You should also practice dancing with false lashes to get used to the feeling long before the day of tryouts. The best technique for false lash newbies is to purchase a lighter fringe, such as the Ardell® 110 Demi lashes, then snipping off the inner 1/4 of each lash so that the strip is shorter and does not reach the inner corner of your eye. You can also purchase lashes that are already shorter and designed to accent just the outer 2/3 of each eye, like the Ardell® Accents lashes. Those are the best ones for lash newbies, since it is the inner corner of the eye that tends to get most irritated when learning to wear false lashes. You can also experiment with lashes that come with glue already embedded in the strip, which work like a stick on, versus the lashes that you will need to glue on. One trick is to let the glue begin to dry on the lash for 30 seconds before you apply each lash; this makes the glue tackier and less likely to smear on as you apply it. There is a great how-to video posted on the M.A.C Cosmetics® website that offers a fantastic visual tutorial.

- **Lashes**. Whether or not you use false lashes, you will need to apply black or deep brown mascara to your lashes (or over your false lashes if you applied those). Use several coats, and be sure to avoid clumps by using an eyelash comb as necessary to separate any lashes that get stuck together. Waterproof mascara is best if you sweat heavily when exercising.

- **Bronzer**. While this step is only optional, many women look great with a light dusting of bronzer applied across their forehead, down the nose, and along each cheekbone for a sun-kissed look.

- **Cheeks**. You will want a soft rosy glow on the apple of each cheek. Brush on a powdered blush, but be sure not to create a doll-like look, so be sure to blend the color well into each cheek to avoid harsh lines. A rose or peach tone is best.

- **Lips**. The best bet for lipstick is to go with a deepest rose or a true red. When in doubt, choose red! Many teams actually require that their dancers wear red lipstick for consistency and visibility from the stands. My all-time favorite red that seems to work with most skin tones is Russian Red by M.A.C Cosmetics®. Another good choice is Charmed I'm Sure (Marilyn Monroe Collection) by M.A.C Cosmetics®. You will want to start with a lip liner to edge around your entire lips, then fill in with color, then finish with a stay-put gloss. One note of caution: You do not want your hair to whip red streaks across your face if your hair brushes against your lips while dancing. That's why it's important to seal your color in with a gloss that will act as a shield for your color when dancing. Test your lipstick and gloss to ensure it is smudge-resistant by dragging a lock of hair across your lips and seeing whether your hair sticks to your lips or smudges the color onto your face. You also need to test to be sure your lipstick and gloss of choice do not come off on your teeth when you speak.

- **Interview portion**. Keep in mind that you might tone the makeup down slightly for the interview portion of the audition if it takes place separately from the dance portion. During an interview, you are generally closer to the judges and will need less makeup. You would apply it the same way, but with a slightly lighter hand and perhaps slightly lighter colors and intensity. Your lipstick can be a few shades lighter than the red you would wear for the dance portion, and you can leave out the sparkle and wear shorter false lashes.

Do you want to see a **VIDEO TUTORIAL** of a woman applying arena cheerleader worthy makeup? Would seeing a before-and-after help you? If so, visit the Arena Cheerleader™ Facebook® page at **www.facebook.com/ArenaCheerleader**, hit "**LIKE**," and then click on the tab for "VIDEOS" to watch a video tutorial given by makeup artist Carla, who will show you step-by-step how to accomplish the right look as she applies makeup to her own face. She has the cutest accent and personality! Carla loves to help women create their makeup looks by teaching them about proper makeup application, so please be sure to leave her a "thank you" comment below her video when you view it!

If you want to take your education further and register for an online course in applying makeup, the University of Makeup offers online courses that teach you how to apply makeup for a flawless professional look. Visit their website for more information.

Eyebrow shaping

Nothing will open up your eyes and give you a polished look more than having your eyebrows properly shaped. Avoid pencil-thin brows; the best brows are thicker towards your nose and end in graceful slim arches. The easiest way to achieve the perfect brow is to go to a professional for an initial shaping, then to continue maintenance on your own with tweezers if you do not want to spend money on ongoing professional shaping. The technique called "threading" is just as effective as tweezing or waxing, and many women say that threading hurts less. Waxing can be less precise than tweezing and threading, but all three methods are fine.

Hair removal

Leg hair, facial hair, stomach fuzz, and armpit hair should be waxed or otherwise removed in preparation for auditions. While that may seem obvious, I have seen candidates forget or neglect to do one or another of these. Don't lose sight of this as you prepare yourself on the day of auditions!

Tanning

Tanning will make almost any body look more toned. The sun-kissed look is usually the best look for most bodies. Pale stomachs tend to look softer and larger next to tanned tummies, so be aware that you might stand out when lined up with other women who have tanned or are naturally tan. Don't aim for an unnatural tan; the goal is to look like you would at mid-summer if you have been sunbathing and generally spending time outdoors, not like a tanning-bed addict.

Tanning beds have been known to increase your risk for cancer, so a safer bet is to have a spray tan or airbrush tan applied, or to use a self-tanning cream at home. Tanning is one of the things that should be experimented with long in advance of the audition, because you must try various methods to find the best one for your skin. The last thing you want is to try a spray tan for the first time the day before auditions, only to find it turns you bright orange!

Be aware of making your body a different color than your face. You do not want your face and body to be completely different colors, which I have seen before. That's not a good look!

Teeth

Teeth should be as straight and naturally white as can be achieved. As explained by Dr. Jon Marashi, *"Your smile is your greeting card. It is the first thing everyone notices when they meet you. It has personality and individuality, just like you. Maintaining a bright, healthy smile will give you the confidence needed for every social setting."*

Dr. Marashi is known as the "Dentist to the Stars" and regularly treats celebrities in his Los Angeles office (**www.goldenmarashi.com**) to help them achieve or maintain star-quality smiles, so he knows the importance of a smile in the world of entertainment.

- **Whitening**. Staining from coffee, tea, smoking, red wine, and other teeth-dulling habits can be reversed or corrected with teeth whitening. Lasers, bleach trays, and special toothpastes can all help you achieve a whiter smile. Smiling is an important part of being a professional cheerleader, so having the whitest teeth you can achieve will help you make the right impression in front of the judges. As a bonus, white teeth will look great in your everyday life, too!

- **Orthodontics**. If you never had orthodontics and your teeth are crooked or crowded, consider orthodontics in preparation for your future auditions. Straighter teeth help you avoid cavities between teeth and can correct bite problems, so it is a good idea to consider teeth straightening for health reasons even if you never plan to audition for a pro dance team. Invisalign® has become the preferred method of treatment for adults who do not want to use traditional orthodontics. Discuss your options with your dentist.

- **Veneers**. When whitening or straightening using lasers, bleaches, or braces aren't the best methods for correcting a less-than-ideal smile, Dr. Marashi sometimes treats his patients by prescribing veneers. He describes veneers in more detail below, along with some great advice for choosing the right dentist if you opt to go this route. Dr. Marashi explains:

"Porcelain laminate veneers are a thin layer of porcelain which are bonded directly to the front of your teeth. Their purpose is to improve the shape, size, color, as well as durability of a tooth. Conditions such as chipped edges, gaps between the teeth, discoloration, atypical tooth shapes, and even crooked teeth can be treated with veneers. When multiple veneers are placed across the front teeth, it is possible to improve the overall appearance of the smile. Celebrities, athletes, business people, and even everyday people have chosen to undergo this procedure. Veneers are sometimes treated as though it is a quick and easy procedure to apply them, but doing it right is actually quite complex. Establishing the proper occlusion, or bite, is the most important factor for long-term success. Choose a dentist who has advanced training in occlusion to ensure you have a stable result. The laboratory the dentist works with is critical for the artistic design of your smile. Ask your dentist which lab he or she uses for ordering the veneers. Find out if the lab is local

and if you can visit them so they can see you in person to help design a beautiful, custom result. Many people have shied away from veneers because they fear the teeth will be too big or too white (i.e. the "Chiclet" squares fake look!). The best dental work is when no one knows you had anything done at all, and many dentists can achieve that look with veneers.

The most important aspect of having veneer treatment is selecting the appropriate dentist. A dentist who belongs to various organizations is not a direct indicator of their clinical skill. Beware of advertisements, as many dentists will show photos of smiles that are not their own work. When selecting a dentist, here are the questions you should ask:

1. *Can you please show me examples of veneer work you have personally done?*

2. *How many veneer cases have you actually done?*

3. *How often do you do this procedure?*

4. *What type of result can I expect?*

5. *Tell me about the dental laboratory you work with.*

6. *What happens if I do not like my result?*

7. *Ask to speak with other satisfied patients who have had the same procedure done.*

Be very wary of online reviews, such as Yelp, or Dr. Oogle, etc. Oftentimes they are littered with false claims. A great dentist with a great reputation will acquire his patients by word of mouth from other satisfied patients. In the end, you always get what you pay for. If the cost seems really low, then quality will likely be the same. This is a long term investment in your health and appearance, so choose carefully."

In summary, do what you can afford to get your smile to its optimal quality. Remember, one of your most important skills as a cheerleader is your ability to engage and excite others with your smile. Bad teeth can be the sole reason you are not selected for a team. I have seen otherwise gorgeous dancers with solid skills who danced with their lips stretched tight in a closed-lip smile because they knew their teeth were not up to par. Unfortunately, the judges won't be fooled.

You can't hide your smile during auditions. Sooner or later, the judges will see your teeth. And if your smile is full of stained, crooked teeth, your chances of making the cut go down dramatically!

Cosmetic surgery

One of the questions you will probably be asked when you are an arena dancer is along the lines of, "Do all pro cheerleaders have breast implants?" This question is crass and often is asked by a less-than-polite individual. It is sometimes a friend of yours making a snide comment or a fan acting inappropriately, but sometimes the question comes from a well-intentioned person who is truly curious.

Most professional cheerleading uniforms are designed to be bust-enhancing. To be seen from a distance, everything in the world of theater and entertainment must be exaggerated, which is why you see ballet dancers, professional ice-skaters, and opera singers in heavy makeup. This is so their features can be seen from afar. Professional arena cheerleading is no different, and everything is accented or slightly exaggerated. Colors are brighter (like having dancers wear red lipstick), features must stand out (such as by using false eyelashes), and uniforms are designed to accent or create curves that can be seen from a distance.

Most people are not aware of the power of a good bra. Wearing the right undergarments can add several cup sizes and fullness to a woman's bust line. In arena dancing, most team members will either be naturally busty, have breast implants, or be temporarily enhanced by wearing a push-up bra or bra inserts when in uniform. Because of this, many fans and bystanders see the team and assume everyone has breast implants, because the odds of having so many curvy women on one team seems too remote, and they are not savvy about the options available in the world of lingerie!

The bottom line is that you absolutely do NOT need to have naturally large breasts OR breast implants in order to fulfill your dream of dancing for the pros. Anyone who tells you differently is ill informed!

What you DO need is to wear the proper undergarments and tools to create some fullness in your bust so that you fit in with the overall look for the team. If all of the team members on the team photocard have well-defined cleavage, then your goal at auditions should be to have a similar look. Here are some tips for creating or enhancing cleavage:

- **Bra selection**. Many bra manufacturers sell push-up bras that will create cleavage and add a cup size. Frederick's of Hollywood, Wonderbra, and Maidenform are three examples, but there's no shortage of great bras out there! I recommend a nude colored bra with removable pads (which means there are pockets where you can add additional padding). Having a bra with convertible straps makes it easier to fit it under different dance tops. Here's another tip: When in a dressing room, make sure to dance in the bra to make sure it is comfortable and doesn't restrict your movement during a dance routine! You are also testing to be sure nothing comes loose or pops out during sharp movements. Other women in the dressing room might stare at you if you dance in the common area of the fitting room, but ignore them and have a little fun with it!

- **Silicone bra inserts**. Many dancers choose to wear silicone bra inserts. These are sometimes affectionately known as "chicken patties" because they resemble a raw chicken breast cutlet! These are soft, pliable bra padding that resemble breast tissue in weight and look. These are sometimes marketed as bra substitutes, but for dancing, these should be worn only in conjunction with a bra, not instead of a bra. Many are sold with an adhesive backing that sticks to your skin. This is recommended because it will prevent the tragic and accidental "flying saucer boobie." Yes, I have seen a chicken patty bra insert fly across the room when the dancer performed a tumbling pass. And yes, it was just as jaw-dropping as you are imagining. I can happily report she played it off and made it onto the squad, but not everyone is going to have that dancer's grace and composure under pressure!

- **Makeup enhancement**. Here's a little-known secret: You can use bronzer powder to enhance or even create cleavage and stomach muscles. This should be done subtly with a light hand, and definitely get a second opinion for your "artwork" before marching it out in front of the judges. The idea is to add some bronzer in a shade or two darker than your natural skin tone to create cleavage and muscles. You brush this carefully between your breasts along the vertical line where your cleavage is (or where it would be). You must blend it in very well and do not go overboard or it will look very obviously fake. You can do the same along your stomach muscle lines, but only if you have some stomach muscles already there. Do not create stomach muscles if none exist— this technique only works to enhance what's already there. For a finishing touch, you can gently brush some shimmer powder on the top swell of each breast to complete the illusion of added fullness.

Cellulite

When candidates realize they will need to audition in dance briefs, which are practically bikini bottoms, the reaction is sometimes horror and dread. Almost all women, even many models, hate looking over their shoulders into a mirror and staring at their rear end and thighs from behind. The thought of dancing in a pair of dance briefs can be enough to make someone choose to stay home on the day of auditions.

The reason so many women focus on their thighs and rear ends—and the reason swimsuit boutiques should seriously reconsider their lighting arrangement in dressing rooms—is cellulite. The bumps, lumps, and sponginess can make even the most confident woman look away from her reflection in frustration. Even women who have reached their weight and fitness goals sometimes can't shake that last bit of tiny fat bulging that we call cellulite.

Luckily, there's some good news for you. The first is that your cellulite is probably nowhere near as bad as you think it is. We tend to see our imperfections with a microscope, while the rest of the world sees us in soft-focus lens. So remind yourself that you are your own harshest critic when it comes to cellulite, to begin to find some courage.

Next, realize that you will not dance at auditions in your bare skin. This is not the beach! You will be allowed (and encouraged) to wear tights or hosiery during your audition. Selecting the correct hosiery will dramatically minimize or even completely eliminate your bumpy lumps. The best brands for hosiery are described in more detail in the "attire" chapter of this book, including which ones to select if cellulite is a concern.

Also, your diet and hydration level will influence the appearance of your skin. Cellulite is exacerbated and worsened when you are retaining water and when you are carrying more fat on your body than is optimal. So losing weight through improving your diet, as discussed in the nutrition section in this book, will help reduce your cellulite. Drinking enough fluids will also play a large role, and cutting salt out of your diet will help you reduce water retention.

Lastly, many women are not aware that the appearance of cellulite can be reduced very effectively by using certain manipulation methods that manually break down the connective tissue fibers that create the pockets of fat on your thighs and buttocks.

The book titled *Beat the Bumps: The Seven Brazilian Secrets to DIY Cellulite Smoothing & Reduction* by Carla Cruz takes readers through a seven-step regimen to combat the appearance of cellulite lumps. To summarize the book, you must regularly push, pull, pound, polish, pinch, pH-balance, and paleo your bumps into submission.

The book explains how a woman can greatly improve the look of her thighs and buttocks by performing some DIY massage and other methods to the affected area. All of the recommended treatments (except the last two) involve manual manipulation. The last two address dietary tips. If cellulite is a problem for you, check out that book to learn some interesting techniques! It will be published in late spring of 2013 by the same publisher that is publishing this book.

Contact lenses & glasses

If you normally wear eyeglasses, do not wear them to auditions. You should leave them off even for the interview portion. Eyeglasses hide your face and are dangerous to wear when dancing. They can create glare in the lights as well. Wear contact lenses or go without if your vision is not too poor.

Colored contact lenses can add some depth and sparkle to your face if done right, but I see colored contacts detract from a woman's appearance more often than I see them improve her look. The colored contacts that tend to look better are the ones with a darker ring around the outside edge of the iris. This is a more natural look. Colors like hazel and light brown look more natural over brown eyes than trying to change to green or blue. When dancers have naturally light eyes, they can enhance or brighten them by using colored contacts. The downside is that colored contacts can sometimes create an "alien" appearance if done wrong, and even when they are done right, they can look distracting when you see view them up close. If in doubt, stick with clear contacts.

Acne & scarring

Active acne flare-ups and acne scarring are very difficult to hide. Acne can occur on the face, chest, and back, and unfortunately these are all areas that are visible during a dance audition. Even though arena dancers are usually over 18 years old and therefore adults, many acne problems follow women into adulthood long after the teenage years, especially with respect to long-term scarring.

There are two ways to deal with acne and acne scarring: Hide it or cure it.

Curing acne is tough to accomplish, which is obvious since an entire industry has grown out of the need. There are countless acne-fighting washes, creams, drugs, and other treatments available on the market. If acne is a problem for you, you have probably tried many or all of these potential cures. You might also have consulted with a dermatologist to find some relief. If you haven't first exhausted these possible cures, you can experiment to see if any of these can help you. A doctor can prescribe topical and oral medications that address acne problems.

My favorite fast-fix cure for an occasional pimple that pops up unexpectedly is to dab a drop of fresh lemon juice on it and then leave it alone. If I have a lemon in the fruit bowl, I don't even cut it open. I poke a tiny hole in it with a knife tip and squeeze out a couple of drops to dab onto the problem spot. This works wonders if acne is not a serious problem and you are dealing with a rare pimple on your otherwise typically clear skin.

Another possible cure is by adjusting your diet, because the foods you eat can be responsible for your acne. Certain foods can trigger acne due to causing hormonal imbalances in your body. Author J.J. Virgin wrote a book about a simple plan that cuts out all of the foods that might be responsible for causing acne. If you want to see if eliminating common trigger foods might help you get clear skin, read her book, *The Virgin Diet*, to learn more.

Laser treatments and other cosmetic medical procedures can erase acne or other types of scarring, but can be expensive. If your scarring is debilitating because it seriously impairs your self-confidence, this might be an avenue to look into. Consult with your doctor or a cosmetic surgeon to discuss your options.

The quickest fix for acne and scarring, if all else fails, is to use the proper makeup. You can use a heavy-duty cover-up and foundation to counteract the look of acne and scars. The only issue is that skin texture can be difficult to camouflage. It is easier to hide color differences. Pits or bumps are more difficult to conceal, but the right products will make a dramatic difference. Consult with an experienced makeup artist at your local mall's makeup counters to see what they recommend for your particular skin.

The downside to relying on makeup is that the heavy concealers and foundation can clog pores and lead to even worse acne. That's why it is better to cure acne using medical treatment than to hide it.

Nails

Nail art is fun, but stick with a plain French manicure or neutral color for your audition. Treat your nails the way you would for a professional interview for a corporate job. Clear, nude, light pink, buff, cream, and French tip are the best choices.

False nails or "pink-and-whites" can be used to give you some length or to correct your nails if you are a nail-biter. Pick a length no more than a 1/2" beyond your fingertips. Shorter than that is even better in case you have to use pom-poms during the audition.

Avoid rhinestones, striping, patterns, glitter, and all bright or trendy colors.

Earrings, rings & other jewelry

Even your jewelry must be carefully selected for the day of auditions. Here is a guideline for what to wear, what to leave at home, and what to avoid:

- **Earrings**. Avoid hoops, long dangling earrings, and large trendy looks. Select a simple pair of studs that extend no lower than bottom of your earlobes. A large sparkly cubic zirconia solitaire on each ear is best, either clear or in the team's main color. A large faux pearl is also a good choice. You can find sparkly solitaires and faux pearl solitaires at any accessories store for under $10.

- **Necklaces**. Leave your necklaces at home for the dance portion. Your neck should be bare. For the interview portion, however, a tasteful necklace should be worn, such as a single or double strand of faux pearls or a pendant on a simple chain. For a pendant, avoid anything that is too large. Your jewelry should complement your outfit, not dominate it.

- **Rings**. Most teams allow their team members to wear one ring. Engaged or married dancers usually choose their engagement or wedding ring as their sole ring. Wear only one ring for your audition, or none at all.

- **Body piercings**. Take out all body jewelry (i.e. belly-button studs), face jewelry (i.e. eyebrow, lip, nose, or tongue jewelry), and any additional ear jewelry if you have more than one piercing in each earlobe. Most teams forbid wearing anything in these additional piercings while a team member is in uniform, so don't distract the judges by showing up with multiple piercings that they know they will have to ask you to hide.

Tattoos

You will want to cover up any tattoos completely if they are visible in your audition outfit. Do this with appropriate theater makeup in your skin tone rather than tape or a bandage. Makeup will look much better than sporting a large bandage!

Chapter 7:
Your Audition Attire

Where do you find the best audition outfits?

So how do you go about planning what to wear? Now that your body, hair, and makeup looks are locked down, it's time to start thinking about what you will wear for the dance and interview portions of the audition.

Sizzling, not sporty!

The main thing to remember is that the look is sizzling, not sporty! You will be competing against professional dancers who have experience auditioning for dance teams. They know the look is polished and glamorous, so don't show up in a ponytail, minimal makeup, and yoga pants!

For some of you readers, this might be obvious advice. But for many audition hopefuls, there is a rude awakening when they walk into the audition only to realize they look naive and unprepared compared to the more experienced candidates.

I have seen amazing dancers with gorgeous looks show up wearing old sports bras in unflattering colors, bicycle shorts, and clunky sneakers. Again, remember, not all judges are willing to give a diamond-in-the-rough the benefit of the doubt!

Top

Selecting your dance top is where you will put the most time and energy. This is where you aim to be unique and memorable. Your dance top is your calling card at auditions; many judges will refer to you by the color you are wearing, such as "the brunette with the yellow top with a fringe." Therefore, you should put a lot of care into what you choose to wear as your dance top.

Here are my thoughts on your different options:

- **Pro-dance-specific top**. There are companies that specialize in designing dancewear for professional cheerleaders. The pro teams use these companies to design and produce the teams' uniforms in bulk, but you can also purchase one-off uniforms to use for your audition. My favorites are Angela King Designs® and DallasWear®.

- **Generic dance top found online**. If you are on a budget, consider getting a dance top online from a retailer like Amazon® or eBay®, then customizing it to look unique. I have run several online searches, and the one search that seems to bring up the best matches for what you need for a dance audition is this one specific search on Amazon.com:

  ✦ Go to **Amazon.com**

  ✦ In the search box, first use the drop-down menu to select "**Clothing and Accessories**"

  ✦ Then type in these exact words in this order: **sexy dance crop top**

  ✦ Hit "**Go**" and browse some amazing dance tops!

- **Bathing suit**. Some candidates audition in bathing suit tops. This is fine as long as the top is comfortable to wear while dancing and doesn't come loose or slip to one side. Triangle-top string bikinis don't hold up too well, but halter-tops are usually up to the challenge. Bandeau tops can be difficult to keep in place unless there is a strap or string that goes up around the neck. It is sometimes more difficult to wear a bra under a bathing suit, so if you need extra lift from a bra or bra inserts (see the section in this book on bras and cleavage enhancers), then perhaps a dance top with greater coverage than a bathing suit is preferable. If you do wear a bikini, be sure to snip off dangling strings to make it less obvious you have a bikini on, and to lessen the distraction that flying strings will cause. You should also consider using body-wear glue such as Hollywood Fashion Tape® double-sided adhesive strips or a spritz of hairspray between you and your top to help it stay in place during the dancing.

- **Sports bra**. Most sports bras are too plain to serve you well on audition day. You don't want to look sporty; you want to look glamorous. Think Las Vegas, not the tennis court! With that said, I have seen some sports bras transform into gorgeous dance tops with a little creative arts and crafts approach. If you are crafty and have sewing skills, you can turn an otherwise ordinary sports bra into an amazing dance top. To get inspired, visit the websites I linked above to see what your target look should be, then design a top out of a sports bra that you can wear at auditions. The first step is to gather or ruche the front so that it gathers into a V-shape at your bust, then work on embellishing the straps or neckline with some sparkle (see below).

- **Sparkle**. I highly recommend getting a top with sparkle already built in, or adding sparkle to it yourself. Metallic fabrics, rhinestones, sequins, beading, and satin piping can all add a touch of shine. Embellish your top so that you shine in the bright lights. Pick one element and stick with it. If you added rhinestones along the neckline, don't also add other sparkle. Pick one method of embellishment and stick to it to avoid making your top look too busy.

- **Cleavage**. Select a top with sweetheart, deep "V" or corset "U" shape to the neckline so that your neckline is enhanced. You want to show off your collarbones, shoulders, and bust to demonstrate to the judges that you would look just as athletic and sexy in the team uniform. Also, please refer back to the section in this book that addresses cosmetic surgery, bra selection, cleavage-enhancing makeup, and silicone bra inserts.

- **Sleeves**. Short sleeves or long sleeves, which will you choose? The answer depends on your arms. Are they toned and lightly muscled? Then go sleeveless or sleeved, your choice. If they are not at all toned, unusually skinny, or very heavily muscled, you might want to wear long sleeves to camouflage them for auditions. You want judges to notice your smile, dance technique, and overall presence. If your arms are noticeably more muscled or much skinnier than the average team member's, this can become a distraction and the one thing the judges remember about you. Keep their focus on YOU, not your arms!

- **Length**. Crop top or longer top, what's best for you? If you cover your stomach, judges will assume you have something to hide. A longer top will also visually shorten your torso, and make the small portion still showing at the bottom look wider than it actually is. For the average pro dancer body, I recommend a top that is cropped to just below your bust (where a sports bra would end). This creates the longest look from briefs to top, elongating the look of your stomach. I have seen some very slim women successfully pull off wearing longer tops that reach down to the bottom of their rib cages or which incorporate a fringe that reaches down past the top. If you have a personal coach or mentor, have them help you make a decision relative to your body type. But if in doubt, go with a crop top. If a couple of fabric strips hang down from a center-tied top, that's fine and a good look as well.

- **Color selection**. Color is where you get to have some fun and make a statement. Pick a bright, fun color that works with your skin tone. Electric blue, cherry red, canary yellow, emerald green, fuchsia, violet, and tangerine are examples of colors that really pop. Solid colors generally look better than patterns, but a pattern will sometimes work on women who have done everything else right. A zebra-striped top on a perfectly groomed candidate with a great body and superior dance skill will help judges remember her as a stand-out ("remember that one wearing the zebra stripes?") but the same shocking pattern could backfire if you were not otherwise fully prepared, by adding one more thing that looked slightly "off" about you. That's why I generally recommend sticking with one bright color that works with your personal complexion, but on occasion I have given a thumbs up to a fun or unique pattern.

- **Get opinions from others**. Not sure which top to wear? Deciding between several top contenders? Here's an idea! Visit the Arena Cheerleader☐ Facebook® page at **www.facebook.com/ArenaCheerleader**. You can post several photos (please no more than four!) and ask the community members to help you pick the best one. You can see their comments, or tally up the number of "LIKES" each one generates. If I happen to be on the page that day, you will get my personal input as well! You can also reach out to your own community of friends and family for opinions.

Briefs

It can be terrifying to learn you will have to audition in front of strangers and other dancers wearing briefs, but don't let that fear make you avoid the issue and get stuck with wearing ill-fitting briefs on the day of auditions because you did not adequately prepare yourself. Shop early, and try various cuts until you find one that works for you.

- **Cut**. Your dance briefs should be high-cut. Wear your briefs up to your hipbones or just above the bones. Do not wear them low at your hip, which I have seen many women do. Briefs never look good worn that low when a woman is dancing. Remember, you are not standing in front of a mirror posing; you are in motion! Wearing your briefs below your hip bones will give the illusion of shorter legs and creates an odd "muffin top" roll in certain positions, even when the dancer is very slim. Even if you feel and believe that wearing your briefs low on your hips shows off your stomach, I have to tell you—in action, it is generally not flattering. Lastly, choose a V-shaped waistband to accentuate your stomach and lengthen your torso.

- **Boy-shorts**. Boy-shorts or bike shorts will shorten the look of your legs and also make your behind look large when you are lined up with other women in smaller briefs. Even though they feel like they cover more and thus make you feel less self-conscious, stick with a classic high-cut brief. If you wear shorts, the judges will assume you have something to hide.

- **Bathing suits**. If you are using a bathing suit as your top, then consider using the matching bathing suit bottom only if it has the same coverage as a typical dance brief. In most cases, you should stick to dance briefs in black or a solid color to go with your bikini top rather than using the bottoms that came with your bathing suit.

- **Thongs**. Do not opt for a thong or Brazilian style cut, even if your behind can sport this look and look good. It will send the wrong message to the judges, and you will stand out from the other candidates as "that woman in the thong." Choose a style with a little more coverage. Yes, I am mentioning this because I have seen someone wear one at an audition!

- **Skirts**. Avoid skirts and fringes unless you had a professional designer with pro cheer experience make your audition outfit. When done right, this can add to the visual appeal of an audition outfit, but I have seen it done wrong more times than I have seen it done right. This is no area for an amateur to dive into without expert assistance.

- **Color.** Stick with plain black as a rule, but matching your briefs to the color of your top is also a good option. Avoid patterns as a general rule.

- **Pins.** Use small safety pins to keep the top of your hosiery or tights just under and below the top of the briefs. Check to make sure that your hosiery or tights do not peek up over the top of your briefs even after intense dancing.

Shoes

Wear jazz shoes to the audition, preferably in nude coloring. Avoid sneakers, boots, bare feet, or other footwear unless you know for a fact that the returning veterans wear such footwear. If auditions are held on grass, you could opt to wear sleek white sneakers instead of jazz shoes, but be sure to also take your jazz shoes so that you can change footwear after you see what the returning veterans are wearing. Your footwear should match their footwear as closely as possible.

Why is the right hosiery your secret weapon?

The right hosiery will make your legs look fantastic and will camouflage your cellulite. If those two reasons aren't enough to make you want to try different brands to find the best one for you, I don't know what will! Here are some great hosiery tips for you:

- **Million-dollar tip!** My number one, million-dollar, "OMG, I can't believe I never knew this" trick for wearing hosiery and tights correctly for dance auditions is this: Always, always, always (I mean without exception) cut a 1" to 3" deep slit down from the top of the waistband, starting at your navel and cutting downward. Stop cutting just before the waistband changes to the sheerer material. Snip, snip! Some cheerleaders that I know even cut off the entire top of the waistband. By doing this, you get rid of the "muffin-top" producing tightness of the waistband, and you also make the hosiery easy to tuck into a V-shaped brief. Try it once and you will never again wear hosiery without first making the waistband slit.

- **Sheer**. Be sure that your hosiery or tights do not have a control top (i.e., avoid the look of wearing tan bike shorts; you do not want a line across your thighs). You also want only a very small cotton diamond in the panty area, because nothing should show outside of your dance briefs during kicks or when bending down, including control top material or white cotton panty area material.

- **Color selection**. Your hosiery should not be a mismatch. Match it to your stomach color. If you are tan, use tan hosiery. If you are pale, go with a matching tone. If you are dark-skinned, use darker shades. Do not wear tan hosiery hoping it will make you look tan if you have not first tanned the rest of your body to match. Do not wear off-white, black, or colored hosiery at a professional dance audition. Stick to a nude shade matching your skin tone as your best choice.

- **Shiny or matte**? In general, shinier tights will accentuate cellulite but will give your legs a great "oiled" look similar to when you wear lotion or suntan oil. Matte will generally camouflage larger thighs better by creating less reflection along your leg lines, but usually offers less snugness and support. Try both and see which works best for you! Taking photos or video and watching the results is sometimes a better way to gauge the look than to just see yourself in the mirror.

- **Best brands**. One of the best brands of hosiery for dancing is L'eggs Sheer Energy® in "all sheer" because it is a slightly shiny pantyhose with a firm elastic feel that hugs your skin snugly and gives you support. For a more matte look, No nonsense® in "sheer to waist" is a good option, but provides less support if flabbiness is an issue for you. Waitresses at the restaurant chain Hooters® wear either Peavey® Hosiery or Tamara® Hosiery, which are also two good options for you to try out (the Tamara® brand is generally rumored to be better quality than the Peavey® brand).

- **One layer or two?** I believe you should wear just one layer of hosiery or tights. However, some women feel that two layers provide greater support and cellulite control. Try wearing two layers to see what you think works for your body. If you wear two layers, keep in mind that the color will darken so choose the color accordingly. If you normally wear tan, you might opt for "light nude" if you are doubling up.

- **Baby powder**. A small amount of baby powder spread all over your legs can help your hose glide on with ease. This is an old ballet studio trick that really works. Especially if you are sweaty, a very light dusting of baby powder can help you slide the tights up your legs without needing to tug and pull as much.

- **Four extra pairs on the day of audition**. Once you find the hosiery or tights that make you feel and look your best, purchase many pairs. You will need them for rehearsing to prepare for auditions and on the day of auditions. Always carry at least four extra pairs with you to any audition. I personally carry even more than that in case someone else needs a pair; you can be the person to save the day for someone!

- **Carry hairspray and clear polish for tears**. In addition, carry hairspray and clear nail polish to stop snags and runs in their tracks. In a pinch, when you don't have time to change into new hosiery, you can apply a dab of nail polish or a squirt of hairspray to freeze the tear before it gets any bigger.

- **No socks, no leg warmers**. Don't wear socks or leg-warmers to the audition. If you choose to wear athletic shoes (even though I advise you to wear jazz shoes, not sneakers) then wear low socks that are hidden under the shoes and don't show.

Take photos in it to compare it to other outfits

If you are deciding between various options for your audition outfit, take photos or video of yourself dancing in each outfit to have a better idea of which one is most flattering on you while standing and also while in motion. Get a second opinion from your family and friends. Be objective and go with the one that makes you look and feel best, not the one you personally like better for other reasons. For example, even if your favorite color is green, choose the yellow top if that is the one that makes you stand out the best.

Rehearse with it on many times

Once you have designed your perfect audition outfit, rehearse with it on many times until dancing in it feels like second nature. This will help you tremendously on the day of auditions.

What is the best outfit for the interview portion?

For many teams, you will wear a different outfit for the interview portion than your dancewear worn for the initial and final dance audition. For teams in smaller leagues, there might not be an interview or you might be interviewed in your dancewear, and so it's possible you will not need to have a separate interview outfit prepared. Be sure to check this out when researching the audition requirements for each particular team.

If the audition info sheet or application gives you interview attire instructions, follow it precisely. If the requirements state that you should wear a business suit, do not assume that a dress shirt and skirt would be appropriate. Wear a full suit, meaning a matching jacket over your shirt.

In general, you will want to look polished and professional. Specifically, this means keeping your attire as close to what you would wear to an interview for a corporate job as possible. There are some pointers below:

- **Attire definitions**. Some audition info sheets will describe the interview attire as, "dressy casual," or "business casual." Others will state, "business attire." Still others might state, "dress nicely." You may even see it described as, "cocktail attire." Unless you have been to the audition or are a mind reader, it's hard to know what each definition means! Here's a list of what to wear for each one:

  + **Casual**: This is the only designation that would allow you to consider denim, but if you are planning to wear denim, I would first contact the team director well in advance of the audition to ask if denim is appropriate. The response might help you decide. If you will wear denim, I would pair your jeans with very high heels or boots and a fashion-forward top worn under a blazer or shirt jacket. Dress up your denim by wearing classic jewelry like a strand of pearls or long necklaces draped around your neck. If you do not wear denim, then an A-line skirt paired with a nice top would be appropriate. Do not wear workout wear such as yoga pants and do not wear a tracksuit. Skirt length can be as short as the tips of your fingers when your arms hang loose.

  + **Dressy Casual**: This is similar to casual, but would include a simple daywear dress, such as a sheath dress in a flattering color. You can also wear slacks paired with a light sweater or knit top, or a skirt with a sheath or camisole top. Skirt length can be as short as for casual wear described above.

+ **Business Casual**: Business casual means workplace-appropriate. This means that you should choose an outfit that does not leave your shoulders bare, and the length of your skirt should not go above the tops of your knees. A safe bet would be a skirt or pair of slacks in a neutral color, paired with a button-down shirt in white or a bright color that flatters you. Stay away from tank tops and camisole tops.

+ **Business Attire**: When the attire specifies business attire, choose a business suit in a neutral color such as black, grey, brown, pinstripe, or taupe. Wear hosiery in a nude shade. If you are wearing black, then you may wear black sheer stockings, but otherwise stick to a nude sheer look. Your suit can be a pantsuit, skirt suit, or sheath dress. Wear your suit jacket to the audition. If you see that no other candidate is wearing a jacket, you can take it off before your turn in front of the judges. Wear a button-down shirt or a colorful top under your jacket. Keep the length of your skirt or dress just above your knees.

+ **Cocktail Attire**: This is where you can safely wear your "little black dress." You can also choose a dress with color or sparkle. The length can be shorter than the other attires described above. You can show a little leg here, but if your dress is short, consider keeping the top more modest to create balance. Separates are also a good choice, such as a pair of skinny slacks with a fashionable top.

+ **Evening Attire**: This is the same as cocktail attire described above.

• **Pantsuit, skirt suit or dress?** Many candidates agonize about whether to wear a skirt, pants, or a dress. If you have outfits available in all three, I would choose the dress or skirt. But pants are fine as long as they fit well and are the correct length (hitting your feet just below your ankles). I see a lot of too-tight outfits at auditions, so be sure that the fabric is not too tight around your hips and that your underwear lines do not show. Be sure to practice sitting down and standing back up to make sure your clothing does not need to be pulled down or adjusted in front of the judges, which is distracting.

- **Shoes**. The best shoes are black, brown, navy, or nude colored. You want them to blend in with the rest of your outfit. If you will wear shoes in a bright color, the color should match and coordinate with your outfit. Open-toed shoes are generally not appropriate in the workplace in a formal setting, but are fine to wear for a dance audition. Do not wear platforms that are very tall or shoes that are overly trendy. Do not wear clunky shoes that can make your feet look ungraceful. Do not wear shoes that have too much sparkle or metal fittings, because they can distract from the rest of your outfit and from you as the main focus. Do not wear clear Lucite shoes with a platform; those are too "Las Vegas" and are distracting. Remember, judges are easily distracted, so keep your footwear simple and flattering.

- **Hair, makeup and jewelry.** Hair, makeup, and jewelry are addressed in detail in the appearance section of this book.

Chapter 8:
Your Mindset & Self

Does your reputation in the dance community matter?

Directors talk. Coaches talk. Employers talk. Team members talk. Dance studios are fertile ground for gossip and intrigue. Chances are, there are only a few degrees of separation between you and someone associated with the team you plan to audition for, even if you are trying out for an out-of-town or even out-of-state squad.

If you were going on a blind date, would you ask around to see if anyone you trust knows him before the date? If you were going to hire someone for a job, would you call a former boss? Of course you would.

Dance team directors have the same curiosity. It's not only smart for them to check out your reputation, but a great way to weed out anyone who might jeopardize the team camaraderie or the sport organization's brand and image.

I personally know of many situations where, as one of the judges, we cut someone at auditions because we had the inside scoop about the person's inappropriate attitude or behavior. There is no "I" in "team," and there is also no "I" in "cheerleader."

If you have a bad work ethic, if you act like a spoiled diva at your dance studio, if you have been dismissed from a team, or if you have a reputation for being tardy or irresponsible, it is time to take a good hard look at your life. There is no better time than now to make amends with people you might have let down or hurt.

Calling up an old coach whom you mistreated to give a simple apology and acknowledgment of your previous bad behavior could work miracles. Showing enemies from previous dance associations that you have grown and changed your ways can make or break you if that person is asked to give a referral and recommendation of you.

Not only is this good practice in preparing for auditions, but in the end, it is good practice in life to heal old wounds and make amends. You might be surprised at how good it will feel, and how far that act of maturity and growth can take you.

What is the team director's biggest fear and how does Facebook affect your odds of making the team?

Believe it or not, the team director's biggest fear is not that he or she might select dancers who later prove not talented enough. They are also not overly worried that they will overlook some "star" who would have been an asset to the team but somehow got cut during the audition process. If someone ends up causing bickering among the team, the director won't lose a lot of sleep. The directors are not even worried that a dancer might lose her fitness level and no longer look good in her uniform.

The directors don't lose sleep over these possible scenarios, because all of those problems are easily fixable. A weak dancer can be camouflaged in routines. A rejected applicant who should have made the team might return the next year to audition again. An overweight dancer can be benched, or cut from the team. Same goes for bickering teammates, or those with attitude problems. A good director will get to the root of such problems quickly, and will move on.

The big fear—the one that makes a director's heart freeze and skip a beat—is that a cheerleader will do or say something that will reflect poorly on the sports organization. A media blunder, or worse yet, a media scandal, can threaten the director's job and the reputation of the team.

America is quick to condemn sports figures, and this includes cheerleaders. Just like political figures, celebrities, Olympians, college athletes, and professional sports players, professional cheerleaders must be very careful about what they say and do in public when they are recognizable as ambassadors and representatives for the team they cheer for.

In this industry, stupidity and bad judgment are dangerous. Immaturity is dangerous. Exploitation of status is dangerous. Romance between players and cheerleaders is in the danger zone as well. Even general cluelessness can be very, very dangerous. And most dangerous of all, is the threat of a cheerleader who would sabotage the image of the team by posing for pornographic magazines or movies.

Because of the possibility of these media and public relations nightmares, pro dance team directors are especially cautious about putting women on a dance team when there is a stronger-than-average chance the individual could put the team at risk. This means that you should look at your Facebook page objectively.

See your web presence through the eyes of the director. Do you post photos of yourself drinking? Wearing skimpy outfits? Being romantically promiscuous? Do you badmouth sports teams? Do you use profanity? Do you show bad judgment?

You are also evaluated during the audition. How do you respond to questions during the interview process? Do you sound intelligent and knowledgeable about sports and the team? If you are on television at a media appearance, will a sound-byte of you speaking make the team look good or bad? When asked simple questions about the team, do you sound embarrassingly clueless?

A director is always on guard about the ever-present dangers and risks of a cheerleader going rogue, saying something inappropriate, or exhibiting bad judgment. Don't do anything at auditions that can mark you as a risky choice. If your social media profiles, web presence, or past activities raise a red flag, this could override an otherwise flawless audition effort. When in doubt, a smart director will keep you off his or her team if there's a chance you could sabotage the team's image.

The time to clean up your image is now; don't wait until the week of auditions. It is also a good idea to brush up on your knowledge of facts about the organization and sports team, to help you sound eloquent and knowledgeable during the interview.

How is auditioning a little like applying for college?

Remember when your high school counselor told you that community service and interesting hobbies make you look good on your college applications? Well, guess what? It works the same way when trying out for a pro dance team.

You will fill out an application for the dance team audition. That application will include spaces for you to fill in your activities, hobbies, employment, awards, accomplishments, and skills. Just like you want to show college admission staff that you are well rounded, you want to do the same thing when applying for a dance team position.

This means that you need to look at your life long before auditions to see if there's more you could give back to the community. Volunteer work and serving on committees helps your community and impresses judges.

If you can't think of anything to say if you are asked about your community work or hobbies, that does not make for a good application (or a great life, if you ask me!). So get some hobbies, do some good in the world, and go out there and generally "show up" more in life. That's another tip from this book that will apply to your life as a whole, not just to your journey in arena dancing!

Positive visualization: What is it and does it work?

There are those who believe that you "jinx" something if you speak with too much confidence about a future event. For example, a lot of people think it's bad luck to tell the world you will win or achieve something before it happens.

But I'm personally in a different camp. I truly believe that we can make miracles happen if we have the right mindset and direct positive energy towards a goal or desire. An over-simplified method for how to channel your positive energy was described in the worldwide hit book, *The Secret*, which was later made into a movie by the same name.

Whether you believe in the power of the "law of attraction" or not, don't you agree that it will help you prepare for auditions to picture yourself out on the sidelines in the team uniform? At the very least, it will help you with your confidence and will get you excited about the journey ahead.

Here are some easy exercises you can do to use positive visualization on your journey to becoming a professional cheerleader:

- **Dream board**. Make a "dream board" or "vision board" by cutting out photos of your favorite team cheerleaders. You can even print out photos from the Internet. Paste or pin these photos onto a small poster board, canvas, or fabric-covered bulletin board and hang it in your room. For maximum effect, cut out your face from photos of you, and paste YOUR face over the face of a team cheerleader! Seeing those images every day will help cement the vision in your mind.

- **Emotional tuning**. At a quiet time, like in bed before sleeping or while taking a walk, vividly imagine what it would feel like emotionally to receive the news that you were selected for the team of your dreams. Try to feel the same feeling of excitement, fluttery joy, and pride of accomplishment that would go through your body if it really happened. See if you can even get your heart rate to speed up, and your face to glow the way it would if you heard that news. Explore the emotion, and see how it affects your whole body. Do not let any doubts or "but you can't" or "but that's impossible" thoughts interrupt you. Squash any negative thought that tries to come in and be "realistic." The exercise it to feel the emotions of success. Do this at least twice per week!

- **Visualization**. In addition to the emotional tuning exercise above, you should regularly practice positive visualization. This can be done right before or after the emotional tuning. Once you get experienced, you can even combine the two, but for most beginners it is best to focus solely on emotions, then solely on visualization. You will want to picture scenes of success. For example, picture yourself looking confident, beautiful, and polished in front of a row of judges. Actually SEE yourself dancing and hitting each move with a confident smile on your face, beaming at the judges. Actually SEE them stare at you, then see them smile in approval and write down high scores in front of them on their score sheet. Watch yourself dance with pointed toes and bold movements. Direct your mind's camera lens to your dazzling smile as the image of yourself sashays onto the dance floor. Watch yourself deliver a confident answer to an interview question. See it the way you might if your life was made into a movie. Then switch and watch it from inside of yourself, as if your eyes were the camera. Choose related scenes, like a scene of you sitting at your computer, drafting a Facebook announcement to your circle of friends to let them know you made it onto the team. See yourself on the sidelines, pom-poms in hand and leg kicked high as you then leap into a turn before hitting a dramatic dance pose. First see that dance scene from the viewpoint of the fan in the stands, watching you, then picture it again from your own eyes, watching your leg kick up in front of your face and the crowd blur into a colorful rainbow as you spin into a pirouette turn. Visualize a phone conversation where you call a new teammate to talk about carpooling to the next game. See how many scenes of success you can come up with and practice visualizing them regularly! The more you do it, the better you will get. I have all of my personal coaching clients do similar exercises on a regular basis, and have witnessed amazing results!

- **Affirmations**. Take this list of questions and statements (and similar ones you come up with!) and write them out in your own handwriting on a piece of paper. Keep that paper somewhere where you will read it every day at least two times per day, such as taped onto your bathroom mirror or to your computer screen. Say these questions and statements out loud every time you see the paper, and then repeat them quietly in your head when you think of it at other times during the day:

  + *"I am courageous because I am moving forward towards my dreams of dancing professionally for the [insert your favorite team]."*

  + *"What can I do today to get closer to my goal of becoming a professional arena cheerleader?"*

  + *"Every day, I am finding ways to improve myself and mold myself into the person I want to become, getting better and better in every way."*

  + *"I am proud of my daily accomplishments towards my goal."*

  + *"I can do anything I dream of, and I can instantly be the person that is the highest and best version of myself, just by deciding to be that self. I choose to be that best version of everything that I am."*

+ *"I have a personal journey to live, and am so excited that dance and cheerleading are a part of that path."*

+ *"I am the architect of my life, and I choose joy, excitement, and passion."*

+ *"I am a good person, and deserve the happiness I feel as I move closer to my dreams."*

+ *"How will this week be the week where I make yet another breakthrough on my path to reaching my professional cheer career goals?"*

+ *"I am grateful to be the kind of person who dreams big and lives life fully."*

+ *"I want to accomplish my dreams because doing so will have positive ripples on the lives of others around me. My accomplishments will help me support the dreams of my family, friends, and others because...[explore the reasons your dreams will help others with their dreams]."*

As you noticed, some of the affirmations are statements and some are questions. When you ask the questions, let your heart answer wordlessly. Do not force a conscious answer. Your subconscious will help you answer the questions by prompting later action on your part. When you make the statements, do so with calm authority and a peaceful, positive energy. Learn to allow joy into your everyday life.

If your beliefs involve prayer or conversations with a higher consciousness, such as God, use that connection with your spirituality and belief system to reach your goal of cheering professionally. This could involve prayer, meditation, journaling, and consultation with ordained counselors of your faith.

You might be skeptical about some or all of the techniques above, but I can tell you this: It can't hurt to use these techniques, and it has helped many people I personally know accomplish phenomenal things in life!

Chapter 9:

Your Application

How to make your application stand out

Your application is an important part of the audition process. Do not take filling it out lightly; most teams will carefully review applications and will likely use them to score or evaluate candidates. Take time to make it shine!

If you have the option, send your application in ahead of time. It is better to have it already in the team director's possession before the day of auditions, because some directors will review early applications, and having your application in her or his hand early might make you more memorable when you show up on the day of tryouts.

Even if you do not submit it early, at least complete it before the day of auditions. You do not want to be filling it out on the morning of auditions. Doing paperwork is not the best use of your time that morning, and your handwriting and grammar might be shaky because you will be dealing with butterflies in your stomach. You have enough going on that day!

Be sure to follow instructions to the "T." This means paying attention to any submission requirements. Be detail-oriented and fill it out completely, marking an "N/A" if something doesn't apply to you rather than leaving a vague blank.

Highlight any past cheer team experience, especially pro teams, media, or entertainment positions. You will want to describe your education background and your professional employment. Include mention of community involvement and any special awards and skills.

Some applications will allow you to attach a resume, while others will state that you must write everything onto the form itself. Again, pay attention to what is being asked of you and comply with all directions. Like with any job application, you are being judged on your skill in completing the paperwork properly and paying attention to detail.

Why hiring a professional photographer can hurt you

Most teams request that you submit a headshot or full-length photograph with your application. It is important that you submit a photograph that is flattering and looks professional. Especially when auditioning for higher-level teams in the NFL and NBA, you will be competing against women who might also be actresses or models. They will have professional photographs from their portfolios to submit, so your photo will be measured against theirs.

Often, a panel of judges will review applications during their deliberation process. Those applications will include your photo, and judges will use that photo to remember who you are and sometimes base final decisions on team selections while viewing the set of photos in front of them.

Needless to say, your photo can sometimes cost you a spot on the team if the photo is not flattering or makes you look like an unpolished candidate next to the other submitted photographs. On the other hand, a great photo can sometimes be the final element that gets you on the team.

Here are some photo tips:

- **Full size**. Submit a full size 8.5" x 11" photo, or (less ideal) attach a smaller photo to an 8.5" x 11" piece of cardstock. Smaller photos can get lost among larger photos when judges lay out finalists on a table. You want yours to stand out, so go for a larger full size rather than a small 5" x 7" photo.

- **Look professional**. Submit a photograph that is taken professionally by an experienced photographer, or the closest thing to it that you can manage on your budget. Do not submit a snapshot, or a photo of you with other people. Do not submit a photo of you with your husband or boyfriend (yes, even if you cut them out of the photo, the floating arm around your shoulders does not look polished!). The key to great photography is LIGHTING. It is all about having proper lighting and using a quality camera. That's why it is best to hire a photographer. But if you must take the photos yourself, be sure that there is a lot of light placed in front of you, behind the camera, so that your face and eyes are lit up. Outdoor shots look best in the early morning or at sunset, when the light shines sideways into your face rather than from overhead. The camera should be a quality one that shoots high resolution photos.

- **Black and white or color?** Either is fine, but if you have both available, I recommend color so that the judges can see your hair color to remember you more easily. You will also be viewed next to color photographs, so you do not want to fade away being the only black and white photo on a table full of bright colors.

- **Make it accurate**. If you have changed your hair color, have grown older, or have changed yourself in some visually obvious way, you should take new photos. If you are a blonde, you should not submit a photo of yourself with reddish hair. If you wear your hair straight for auditions, do not submit a photo of you with curly hair. If you have headshots that were taken when you were eighteen, do not submit them when auditioning in your late twenties.

- **Head or body?** The application instructions might specify whether you should submit a headshot or full-length shot. Follow the instructions precisely. If neither is specified, you should submit both. Many models and cheerleaders use a full length shot with a headshot embedded in a corner of the photo. That way, the page contains both a headshot as well as a body shot. You can also submit two separate photos, but it is best if both shots are combined on one page. Your body full-length shot can be in a bathing suit, dancewear, or casual clothes, but when in doubt, use one where you are in dancewear.

- **Label**. Be sure to label the back (or front) of your photo with your full name (first and last). Often, a photo will get separated from its application in a stack and you do not want yours to go missing.

- **Smiling or sultry**? A sultry look can look dynamite, but when in doubt, go with a high-energy smiling shot. I have seen a few photos where I advised the candidate to use the serious, intense version, but those were rare occasions and I usually recommend a smile because a lot of judges want to know you can create that joyful and energetic look. If you submit two photos, then you can even submit both looks—such as a smile in your full-length shot, and a sultry look in your headshot.

Always check the background and references for any photographer you think of working with, and contact prior clients for a personal referral. Shopping around is a great idea. You can also check to see if the photographer who shoots the images for the team you plan to audition for also offers freelance photography services for individuals.

If you decide to hire a professional photographer to take photos of you, please be aware of this potential danger: Many photographers (especially ones who volunteer to do your photos or do not charge you too much) ask you to first sign their "standard" paperwork before they take your photos. I have seen many photographers' release forms incorporate contract language that essentially gives the photographer ownership of the photographs, or joint ownership with you. Many times, it is worded in a way that allows the photographer to sell the images of you to other parties. Some may tell you that they require you to sign it or they won't photograph you.

While this may seem routine and not overly risky, you should carefully read such contracts before signing anything. Most photographers charge an average of $200-$300 for a two to three hour photo shoot. If any photographer tells you that the value is much higher than this, and tells you that he or she will give you a "great deal" by shooting you for free as long as you let them use the images, this is not a good deal for you. The value of those images can be much, much higher, and you would have no control over where they end up. Think about that before giving someone ownership of your photos and image.

This may not seem like a big deal, but how would you feel if in a few years you see your photo on the cover of a racy book? Or as the model on a dating website? Or in a poorly-produced swimsuit calendar? All without your knowledge or permission? I have seen many trusting women sign away their image rights without even knowing they agreed to allow such use of their photos.

Even if you think you know and trust the photographer, do not sign a general release to your images. If the photographer wants to someday use your photos, he or she should have to come back to you and negotiate a fair arrangement. If he or she wants to use an image on a portfolio website, you should be asked for specific permission that indicates which photo and where it will be used.

I personally believe these issues are important enough that you should seek another photographer if the one you plan to work with wants to own the rights to your image and the photos.

Here is some sample language you can use to protect yourself when hiring a photographer (if you want to download this language in a Microsoft Word® format so you can cut and paste it into other documents, you can download it for free if you join the Arena Cheerleader™ mailing list at **www.ArenaCheerleader.com**):

[Your name] (referred to herein as the "Model") and [Photographer company name] and [Photographer individual's name] (referred to collectively herein as the "Photographer") intend this to be a contract for services and each considers the products and results of the services to be rendered by the Photographer for the Model hereunder (referred to for purposes of this Section as the "Work") to be a "work made for hire" or "work for hire" by the Photographer as an independent contractor for the benefit of the Model. The Photographer acknowledges and agrees that the Work (and all rights therein, including, without limitation, copyright) belongs to and shall be the sole and exclusive property of the Model and agrees to provide the Model with all images generated in connection with the Work. The Photographer agrees not to reproduce, distribute, publicly perform, or display in any manner any materials developed in connection with the Work, including in particular on any web site or portfolio, without the prior written consent of the Model in connection with each particular instance. The Model's name, likeness, voice, biographical details, testimonial, or photograph may not be used by the Photographer for any purpose, including marketing, advertising or licensing such rights to others, without the prior written consent of the Model. In the event of any inconsistency between the foregoing and any other agreement, oral or written, between the parties, the foregoing shall control.

If you are later asked for permission to use one of your photos somewhere, such as in a portfolio, you can borrow this wording when giving the photographer your permission (this can be sent via email):

You have asked me for permission to use the photograph attached to this email in your portfolio that appears at the following domain: www.[PhotographersPortfolioSite].com. You have my permission to display that specific image on that particular web site, but you may not publicly display my name or contact information. This permission is revocable, meaning you can display the photo in that manner unless and until I notify you otherwise. Thank you for including me in your portfolio.

Of course, please check with your own legal advisor to be sure you are protecting yourself adequately. The information above is for educational purposes only, and should not be interpreted as legal advice. There is no "one size fits all" when it comes to contract language!

Chapter 10:

Your Audition Day

What to expect on the day of auditions

Congratulations! When the audition day is around the corner, you should feel really excited, especially if you have taken the steps in this book to prepare for the big day. Nothing looks better during a tryout than confidence and energy. Be proud of yourself for all of your preparation, and show up with your head held high and a sparkle in your eye!

What are the typical components of a pro cheer audition?

Every team runs the audition process its own way, so there is no hard and fast rule about what to expect. Some teams even change their procedures from year to year. That's why you should always be prepared for any possibility. That way, you will not be caught off guard if the team does something unexpected.

Here are some typical audition elements:

- **Initial welcome**. The day will probably start with some sort of introduction. You will be told what to expect, how the day will run, and will likely hear the biographies for key personnel and the choreography instructor.

- **Warm-up**. There may be a group warm-up, or you might be instructed to warm up on your own. Be aware that you are already on display.

- **Choreography**. The group will probably be taught a group routine. Some teams may skip this and prefer to see only solo routines choreographed by each candidate. But the typical experience includes learning the same routine as every other candidate. Some of the staff members watching this portion might be judges—you never know. Even while learning, be sure to exude confidence and showmanship.

- **Practice**. Although you will feel like there wasn't enough time given to you for practice, you will have at least some time to practice and polish the steps before you are expected to perform for the judges. Many teams will also give you grooming touch-up time after or concurrent with the time designated for practice.

- **Judging**. The judging component is where you get to dance and perform in front of a panel of judges. This can be in groups of two or three, or solo by yourself, depending on how that team structures its audition format. You might be asked to dance with pom-poms or with bare hands, with an open public audience or no audience at all, in front of the other candidates or by yourself in a room separate from the other hopefuls, and you might have to perform the routine more than once. There might be videocameras in the room, so do not let that distract you. The format can vary from team to team and even year to year, so walk in with an open mind about what to expect.

- **Interviews**. Not all teams have formal interviews. Some teams' judges might just ask you a few questions right before or after the dance portion, with you standing out on the dance floor. Others might set up an interview room where you will sit in front of a panel of judges. Interviews can take place the same day as the preliminary audition, or might take place on a separate designated day. For the teams that include an interview portion, this might be solely for finalists who make it to a final round rather than for the entire pool of applicants. Brush up on your personal introduction, knowledge of current events, knowledge about the team and league, and general sports knowledge.

- **Solo routines**. Not all teams will require you to perform a solo routine. Like with interviews, this might be reserved only for the candidates who are selected for a final round. Some teams request that you wear a different outfit for your solo, while others will ask that you wear the same costume as you did for the group performance. This element can take place on the same day as the first round, or at a later date, such as the following day or a week later.

- **Final rounds**. Not all teams have a final round, because some teams will hold only one main round and one cut. It generally depends on the size of the turnout of candidates. The more applicants there are in relation to the size of the final team, the more rounds of cuts the team will probably make. The final round can consist of the same routine as the initial round, or a new routine. It might be the same routine from before, but with added 8-counts to make it longer. You might perform in groups of two or three, or solo, or a combination of group and solo work. Be prepared for anything, even impromptu interview questions when you take the floor.

- **Media interviews**. Do not be caught off guard if you see media in attendance. Local news stations, photographers, and newspaper reporters will probably be in attendance for the audition, especially if it is for a major league team. Never assume that you can quietly audition for the team without anyone at work or in your family finding out—it's very possible your family, friends, and coworkers will see you on the news that night! During registration, you will most likely have signed a liability waiver and photography release that gives the team the right to photograph you and use those photos on their website, in video, or to give other parties the right to those images.

- **Veteran candidates**. Some teams give veteran returning team members a "pass" on auditioning and allow the vets to remain on the squad without re-auditioning. Other teams make veterans audition side by side with new rookie candidates. Yet still other teams opt for a hybrid method, where veteran candidates can skip the first preliminary round, but may show up automatically at a later round. It is a good idea to find out which way the audition you attend is organized, so that you have a better feel for who's your competition. There is usually a lot of tension in the air when veteran candidates walk into the audition room for the first time when they were not there for the earlier round. Many candidates do not realize that veterans sometimes get to skip the early rounds, which gives a false sense of the talent level in the room at the start of the audition. It can throw people off their game to realize that they misjudged the number of top competitors. Here's an important note: Do not be intimidated by the returning veterans! Instead, LEARN from them by watching how they dance, how they interact, and how they carry themselves. You should emulate their body language and grooming as much as possible.

- **Additional post-audition cuts.** Some teams will select a group of women to join the squad, but will reserve the right to continue with cuts during a training period that could last a few weeks or the entire pre-season. For those teams, the audition doesn't truly end until the team's management announces that the cutting period is over. Other teams will only cut team members for good cause, such as absences or bad behavior.

How are auditions scored?

Scoring and judging methods vary from team to team. There is no standard method. On the Country Music Television reality series *Dallas Cowboys Cheerleaders: Making the Team,* which follows the audition process and making of the annual Dallas Cowboys Cheerleaders squad, the team director instructs judges to score each candidate with either a "yes," "no," or "maybe." Other teams follow a similar format. Some teams use numerical scoring instead, which can be on a 1-10 or 1-5 scale. Yet others follow other scoring conventions.

Some team directors choose not to use scores at all, but have the judges write down only notes and comments. Some teams are selected subjectively based on discussion among management and judges, while others weigh the numerical scores heavier when selecting or whittling down the candidates.

For teams that use numerical scoring systems, the judges might give one overall number for each candidate, or might give separate numerical scores for specific categories, such as one score for dance and another for grooming. The formulas for averaging the scores between categories, and the decision to weigh one category higher than another (for example, whether to weigh a dance score higher than an appearance score), also varies depending on what the team's management decides to do that year.

The main takeaway here is that you should NOT agonize over how the selection system will work at your particular audition. Chances are, the system is not publicly described like the one on the *Dallas* show, so you might never know exactly how the final decisions are made.

You should focus on doing your own personal absolute best, and don't stress over how the scoring and selection technicalities operate. Even if you know how they work, it would be extremely difficult to successfully "game" the system or have an advantage simply by knowing how the decision process works. Your best bet is to go out there and CRUSH IT, giving your top performance so that you increase your chances of getting selected, regardless of how the scoring is done.

What should you take with you?

An audition can be an all-day affair, lasting from early morning through the evening. For smaller teams, this can be shorter, but be prepared to stay all day in case the turnout is larger than expected.

Here is a packing list for you to use, which you can customize to fit your personal needs. If you want to download this list in a Microsoft Word® (so that you can customize it) or Adobe® PDF format (so you can print it out), you can download it for free if you join the Arena Cheerleader™ mailing list at **www.ArenaCheerleader.com**.

- **Audition bag.** Pack everything into a duffel bag or small rolling suitcase. Do not show up with multiple bags or small bags hanging off of you. Fit all smaller bags, such as makeup bags and hair styling tool bags, into one large bag that consolidates everything you need. Be sure to attach a luggage tag with your name and phone number on it in case your bag gets lost.

- **Small baggage lock.** Bring one of those small combination suitcase locks that are sold for airplane travel. Make sure it requires a combination that you can easily remember, not a key. You can use this to secure your bag during the audition. There are a lot of people at auditions, and you want to make sure your belongings are secure when you are not with your bag. If you have heard rumors of problems with theft at that particular audition, you may even want to bring a small cable like those used to lock up bicycles so you can secure your bag to a railing.

- **Warm-ups.** Wear a tracksuit or warm-ups over your audition outfit when you arrive. You can also put this on later to stay warm between rounds.

- **Clear packing tape.** You will likely be given an audition number that you will pin onto your outfit. In case this number tears or starts to get wrinkled, you can use the clear packing tape to do some restoration work.

- **Safety pins.** This is for your number in case you are not provided with enough pins, as well as emergency outfit repairs.

- **Bottled water.** Bring much more water than you think you will need. Remember, you will be dancing all day, and dehydration can sneak up on you and zap your energy. Don't count on drinking fountains being conveniently near or available. You do not want to waste practice time waiting in the line for the drinking fountain. It is also difficult to drink more than a few mouthfuls at a time when drinking from a fountain, and the water quality might be lacking.

- **Snacks.** Pack snacks that will not be messy to eat, and that will not give you a sugar crash. Unsalted nuts, protein bars, cut-up fruit, and canned protein smoothies make convenient and healthy snacks.

- **Mirror.** Bring a large mirror in case there are none provided or the public mirrors are crowded.

- **Makeup.** Bring your full set of makeup, not just touch-up items. Even bring your foundation, in case you have to wash your face and start from scratch due to excessive sweating during the preliminary round.

- **Hair tools and products**. Bring your full set of hair products (hair spray, shine spray, gel, mouse, etc.) and styling equipment (curling iron, flat iron, etc.).

- **Hot tool sleeve.** If you will bring a curling or flat iron, consider buying one of the heat-guard cover/sleeves that allows you to pack your curling or flat iron before it fully cools.

- **Tissues**. Bring tissues and baby wipes.

- **Backup outfit**. Bring your audition outfit, of course, but also a backup outfit in case you need to change. You can even bring two extra outfits, such as your "runners up" outfits that didn't make the final cut when you selected your final outfit from all of your options.

- **Hosiery**. Don't forget your tights or pantyhose! And bring several extra pairs. You will probably get at least one run that day.

- **Clear nail polish**. Bring some clear polish to dab onto pantyhose runs to stop them in their tracks if you don't have time to change them and the run is very small.

- **Toothbrush and toothpaste**. A box of mints is a good idea as well. Do not bring any chewing gum. Most people look tacky or unfriendly when chewing gum.

- **Deodorant**. Choose a clear "no mess" roll-on or solid over the spray kind. Get the kind that advertises "no white marks" so that you do not have powdery-looking armpits.

- **Small towel**. Like when going to the gym, a workout towel is a must for drying off sweat.

- **Music**. If you prepared a solo routine, throw a copy of your music on a CD into your bag, just in case you have the opportunity to perform it. You should also take it with you on a small thumb drive as an MP3 file if you can. You can also pack a small inexpensive MP3 player and headset to listen to it during your free warm-up time or during long wait times if you need something to calm your nerves. Be sure to remove the headset if you are within eyesight of the judges.

- **Identification**. Bring your identification and a copy of your medical insurance card. It is also a good idea to jot down any medication allergies on your insurance card copy in case of an emergency.

- **Cash**. Bring a small amount of cash to cover the application fee (if any) and contingencies like parking fees, lunch, and emergency cab fare.

- **Extra copy of your application**. Even if you sent your application in early, bring an extra copy of it with you, along with an extra headshot. If your application got lost in the shuffle somehow, you do not want to fill one out from scratch.

- **Extra shoes**. Bring an extra pair of dance shoes, in case the floor surface creates issues with your original pair or in case your original pair breaks.

- **Phone**. If you bring a cell phone, be aware that your belongings will probably not be secure or under your control while you are dancing. Think twice before bringing an expensive smart phone with you. Consider borrowing a less-expensive phone to have with you for the day of auditions to avoid major issues in case of theft.

Lots of down time

Expect a lot of down time. Utilize your down time to rehearse the dance further, chat with other candidates, stretch, and touch up hair and makeup. Do not let the down time make you nervous, and use that time to drink water so that you remain hydrated, and to eat snacks so that you keep your energy level up.

Always be in audition mode

Your audition begins when you are within eyesight of the audition location. You are always on display, even during break times and the warm-up period. Keep in mind that you are being judged at all times.

This means that every minute counts, even when you are at the registration table. You should be as friendly and polite to the staff person who checks you in and gives you your number as you are to the judges. The registration staff might have the direct ear of the team director. For all you know, the team's choreographer was the person who checked you in!

Do not chew gum or chat loudly on your cell phone around other people. Gum chewing makes a person seem less classy, and it can also make you look unfriendly. Speaking loudly on a cell phone in public can appear rude.

All members of the organization, photographers, media personnel, and other co-applicants should be treated with courtesy and respect. Always be polite; you never know who's watching!

Learning the choreography

The choreography will likely be taught at a fast pace. This can make a lot of dancers nervous. It is stressful enough to be on display in front of judges, but now you will have the added stress of speed-learning a complex dance routine.

Do your best to keep up, and try to keep your face positive and calm (even if you are frustrated and worried on the inside). Many judges preview the group during the learning portion, so it is important to stand out as a star even during this early part of the day.

Try to perform as full out as possible every time that the teacher has the group practice to music. Make it a rule that if the music is on, you are on 100%. It will tire you out more than just marking the steps, but it will help your body learn to automatically perform the dance in full-out game mode. If you practice weakly by marking it, you will probably end up looking less than 100% in front of the judges when it counts. If you prepared adequately before auditions by getting yourself in tip-top fitness condition, then it won't be as grueling to push yourself to go full out all day.

If your double-turn pirouettes are not clean and controlled, consider doing a single-turn pirouette instead where the routine includes turns. Be as precise in your arm and leg motions as possible. Be aware of placement for each position by watching the choreographer and teaching assistants carefully.

Be sure to use your shoulders and hips to add a flirty sass to the moves that call for it. Listen to the instructor. If she or he says that a certain move should be performed with attitude, be sure to add in some flair!

Keep your movements big, meaning that you should dance as if you own the space around you. Do not be bashful or timid with your motions. Every cell in your body should exude confidence and fun energy while you dance. For inspiration, do a search on **Youtube.com** for professional cheerleaders dancing at games. Many fans post videos of halftime and other performances. Watch how the cheerleaders mesmerize the crowd with their big, bold movement. Emulate it!

Small details, like pointing your toes and paying attention to your hand position, are critical. But your overall showmanship is far more important then the small details!

Why do your smile and body language matter so much?

The quality and genuineness of your smile are critical factors for your success. Your smile truly determines the impression you make on the judges. As a cheerleader on the team, you will be expected to smile for most of the time you are in the public eye. The judges want to know you can handle that responsibility and that you have the capacity to look joyful and excited even when under intense pressure.

A cheerleader who looks nervous during a halftime performance will not look right. Similarly, a face furrowed in deep concentration is not fun to watch either. Worse yet, no one wants to see a cheerleader who looks terrified! So avoid any of these expressions out on the dance floor.

But a smile without confident body language cannot look genuine, so you are going to have to address how you stand, walk, and speak during the entire audition process.

So I'm going to share a secret weapon with you about body language. It's an amazing and effective tool. I've been using this technique for much of my life, but never really realized that I did, or understood the reason it works so well, until I heard a presentation about it by social psychologist Amy Cuddy. Her research on body language reveals that we can change other people's perceptions—and even our own body chemistry—simply by changing body positions.

You heard that right; you can change how you feel by first changing how you are standing. Amy teaches how "power posing"—standing in a posture of confidence, even when we don't feel confident—can affect testosterone and cortisol levels in the brain. She explains, "Don't fake it 'till you make it. Fake it 'till you become it." If you want to learn the science behind this theory, listen to her TED® Talk titled "*Your body language shapes who you are.*" It is 20 minutes long and worth every minute, but if you are short on time, then I suggest you at least watch from the 17:00 mark for the last three minutes.

If you practice nothing else before auditions, practice smiling while under stress. Also practice walking, standing, and speaking with confidence even when you feel scared or intimidated inside. Like Amy teaches, fake it 'till you BECOME it! It's harder than one might think, but a skill that will serve you well for life.

How your facial expressions can sabotage your performance

Before I cheered for the pros, I was an instructor for the Universal Cheerleaders Association. That job involved judging many high school cheer and dance competitions. I was an instructor for several years, and over those years I witnessed an evolution in the facial expressions cheerleaders and dancers used during routines.

Somehow, it became in style to add scowls, power play movements like bicep flexing and air slashing, and even some movements that I could have sworn looked like something a mobster on television would motion to offend another character on the show. In addition to these odd menacing "we are number one and you better step off" type dominance body language, I also saw an increase in exaggerated winking, open mouthed surprised expressions, shocked faces, attitude, "kissy-face," pouting, goofy sticking out of tongues, and just general "over-acting."

Because this type of facial play became so common at the high school level, I did see some spill over into the pro world at auditions. Needless to say, most of this does not go over well at a professional-level audition.

Go easy on adding facial expressions. Your performance should be at least 90% smiling, with the other 10% adding a little bit of sass in the form of opening your smile wider for a moment or two, or perhaps winking once or twice in your entire routine. Keep it mainly "smiles" and you won't have to worry about coming across as "over the top" or silly.

The last type of facial expression that you should never show is to lip sync along to the song. I have seen this a few times, and it never looks good. An arena cheerleading audition is not an air band routine or karaoke. Do not act like a rock star, because the judges are not looking for pop stars—never sing along to the song while you dance.

Should you show off your gymnastics?

Showing off gymnastics skills at an audition is a tricky thing. It can easily backfire on you. I recommend doing one clean pass (such as a series of back-handsprings or an aerial cartwheel) during your entrance or solo ONLY if you can nail it consistently and gracefully, have no issues on hard floors, and can perform well under pressure.

I have also seen a successful single back-handspring or standing back-tuck performed during the "freestyle" portion of a group audition routine. Those work well when the candidate lands cleanly and immediately picks up with the dance movements. This is not the time to whip out your rusty grade-school gymnastics skills. If you are not in current practice, don't risk the possibility of injury, a shaky landing, distance misjudging, or general awkwardness.

If you are an experienced gymnast and decide to perform gymnastics at the audition, don't show off your toughest trick. Stick to something clean and reliable. To many of the judges, a series of three back-handsprings will look just as impressive as a double-full layout. Many will not have the eye or experience to differentiate between the different gymnastics flips, so stick to whatever you can do without concentrating too hard. Believe me, you will need your focus for the next stage! I have seen candidates freeze after throwing a tumbling pass, forgetting the audition routine because they were so focused on the gymnastics. Don't let that be you!

Top tip for what to do when your turn on the floor is only minutes away

One of the most terrifying moments during an audition is that one- to four-minute period when you are almost to the front of the line during the solo or small group portion. For many dancers, this is the time when the world starts closing in, heartbeats get frantic, and breathing becomes difficult. You watch as the number of women in front of you dwindles to nothing, knowing you are next on the floor, your entrance mere seconds away. You might even have this flashing thought, "What would happen if I make a run for the door and never look back?"

My top tip for that moment is this:

First, take a deep breathe.

Second, pull your shoulders back and stand in a pose of confidence, whether you feel it yet or not.

Third, get that performance smile on your face, even if it is a few minutes early. And keep it there until it's your turn to enter.

Last, in those last couple of minutes, look at the judges. Watch their faces. Face your fears, and know that those faces will be watching you momentarily. Then tell yourself, "They want me to do my best. Those judges want every one of us out here to give our best audition. Nobody on that panel wants me to fail; everyone is supportive and rooting for me." Create a feeling of excitement. Imagine that the judges know you personally, and that they know you are a great dancer and are excited to watch you perform for them. Imagine that you have friends at that table. And when you walk out there, smile at those friends, connect with them, and shine for them.

What to do during your floor entrance

Your entrance can be one of the most important parts of your audition. You are already on stage even when you are waiting for your entrance, such as when standing in line or being next in line. Personally, I jot down my first impression of a candidate while I watch each one come out onto the floor.

During your entrance, you have no choreography to worry about. You are not yet dancing or performing the 8-counts. You can concentrate less on dance steps and 100% on your presentation of your pure self.

Make your entrance shine. Don't walk timidly on and then turn it on only once the music starts... it is too late to make a first impression at that point. Instead, sashay your way gracefully onto the dance floor with a subtle jazz-style walk (pointed toes, light on your feet, shoulders up and back, stomach held tight, dazzling smile). Use your shoulders to communicate your confidence and energy. Exude the same energy you would show if you were actually on the team walking out in front of the fans. Chin up and carry your neck stretched elegantly tall!

Make eye contact with every judge on the panel, smiling at each one as if he or she were an old friend you were excited to see. Truly CONNECT with your eyes. You can even wink at a judge or two but don't overdo it!

Take your start place on the floor with a final flourish, such as sharply drawing your leg into the beginning pose. As you stand waiting for the music, many of the judges will be evaluating your appearance and body, so make sure to stand in a flattering pose of power and not meekly or shyly. Judges want to know how you will act when you are just walking around or standing at promotional events, not just when you are dancing. That's why your demeanor during non-dancing portions of the tryout is so important.

What to do if you forget the choreography

Commonly, a candidate will lose concentration or her memory will fail during the performance. This can be caused by any number of distractions or even just stress and fear. Sometimes it becomes a domino effect, with one dancer losing her steps and causing the other dancers to falter as well.

If this happens to you, try your best to keep your face positive and confident. Pose in a flattering position long enough to get your bearings, then catch up to the routine. If you are completely at a loss, then just start over from the beginning or from where you left off and keep dancing as if no one else is on the floor with you.

The judges are looking for confidence and the ability to keep your cool, so do your best to stay composed no matter what happens, and to recover as best you can from any memory lapses.

How to exit in a way that maximizes your score

No matter how much you want to run off the floor as fast as you can after your time in the limelight ends, do not give in to that flight instinct! When you strike the final pose, you will probably feel elation, relief, mortification, or a combination of those and similar emotions. If you prepared for your audition well by following the prep advice in this book, hopefully you will feel only elation and no mortification! But feeling relieved is a given.

But despite your relief, do not slump into relaxation mode when you end your performance. Keep that confident and dazzling smile on your face, and connect again with each judge with your eyes. Wait patiently for the person cuing the candidates to release you or your group from the floor before moving off. Stand in a flattering pose while you wait, similar to a pose you would see on a team headshot, such as standing with one leg slightly bent and one hand on your hip.

When you are released, walk off with confidence, gliding off stage similarly to how you entered. Remember, you are always on stage, even when the music stops, and even after you have walked off.

Interview answers that get high scores

Why do you think a team would want to add an interview component for their pro cheer audition?

You guessed it. It's because the judges and team management need to evaluate how a candidate would perform when interviewed by the media and to learn about that woman's personality and outside interests.

In addition to being evaluated on your knowledge of sports, the league, the team, and current events, you are also being judged on your ability to communicate clearly and intelligently.

Do not panic! There are ways to prepare for the interview to increase your chances of making a great impression. Here are several tips to help you:

- **Toastmasters®**. For general practice speaking to groups and in a presentation setting, participate in a local Toastmasters® group. These groups meet specifically to have members take turns presenting short speeches in front of the other group members, and to receive critique. Perform a Google.com search to find a Toastmasters® chapter in your city.

- **Sports knowledge.** In an earlier section of this book, I already discussed how sports savvy you need to get prior to auditions. Be sure to brush up on your sports rules knowledge.

- **League knowledge.** You should go to the league's website to learn about the league as a whole. You should know who won the previous year's championship, and you should read the press releases on the site to learn about recent newsworthy league events. You should know how many teams are in the league, and you should be familiar with the names of other cities and teams in the league.

- **Team knowledge.** The team website is a great resource. Study the staffing lists, so that you know the name of key personnel in the organization, such as coaching staff and executive office staff. You should know the name of the team's owner, and any key events in recent team history. You should know the names of the team's starting players.

- **Current events.** Review CNN.com and other news websites to get a feel for current events.

- **Introduction.** You should have a 30-second introduction prepared in which you state a salutation ("good evening"), your full name, your dance background (such as teams you were formerly on), your current profession (i.e. student, store manager, stay-at-home mom, teacher, actress, etc.), your hometown, and a "thank you" to the judges or expression of your excitement to be there tonight. You can mix it up and change the order of these elements, or substitute other personal tidbits in place of these suggestions. I have included an example personal introduction below:

> *"Good evening everyone, my name is Carla Smith. I'm a former dancer for the Newtown Teamsters, and have been dancing ballet for the last five years. I'm currently working as a project manager for a construction company. Newtown is my hometown, but I am excited to have moved here to Anytown last year and would love to become a part of the Anytown Dancers. Thank you for your time tonight."*

To help you prepare, practice giving answers to the questions below to a friend or family member until you can deliver answers confidently and eloquently. Sample answer prompts are included, but this is where you should not stick to the script, of course! The key is not just to be yourself, but to be the best version of yourself. It is acceptable to pause for a couple of seconds before jumping in to your answer, but don't let the pause get uncomfortably long.

Here are some sample questions:

- **"Who is your favorite player on the team?"** You can name a player, or explain that you have several favorites and name them with a short explanation about why they are your favorite.

- **"What could the team have done better last season?"** You should know how the previous two seasons went. There will be a lot of commentary out there already from sports anchors on local channels discussing the team's performance, so you should be familiar with the general consensus about how the team could improve the coming season.

- **"Have you been to any of our home games before?"** Be honest. If yes, describe what you enjoyed and why that prompted you to audition. If not, explain what other games you have attended or cheered at, and what you love about attending sports games in general. You can also explain why you have not been to the team's games, such as living in another city or difficulty in getting tickets.

- **"Why do you want to be a professional cheerleader for our team?"** This is where you can talk about the qualities that attracted you to the team, such as a reputation for quality, a childhood dream, or a general desire to be part of a sisterhood of successful and beautiful women.

- **"In your opinion, did the football team have a good season last year?"** Again, here is where your Internet research will pay off.

- **"Have you ever faced a big challenge, and how did you handle it and learn from it?"** Think about this question before auditions, because this is a common interview question. This is one you will often hear at any job interview, and a dance team job is no exception!

- **"Tell us a little bit about yourself."** This is where you can elaborate on the general introduction you gave earlier. Talk about hobbies or an interesting fact about your life, such as being raised in a foreign country. You can also describe community service activities you are involved in.

- **"What do you do for a living?"** This question allows you to expand on your job description, or to elaborate on your studies at school. If you are a student, you can discuss what you plan to do after you graduate.

- **"Tell us about someone who has impacted your life."** This can be a parent, a role model, a mentor, or a friend.

- **"Who is your biggest role model?"** Again, this can be family or a friend, or even a celebrity or public figure.

- **"What is one of your most exciting memories?"** Think about a time in your life when you did something exciting that would be interesting to talk about. Tell a story, but keep it short.

- **"Do you think cheerleaders are good role models for young girls who come watch our games?"** This can be a tricky question, especially if the team uniforms are revealing or controversial in any way. Think about this type of question ahead of time, so that you have a thoughtful and positive answer.

- **"Who is the football organization's President?"** This question and similar questions require that you study team and staff rosters carefully before the audition.

- **"If a fan comes up to you after we lose a game and tells you he thinks the team is really terrible this season, how would you respond?"** This question tests your ability to be a positive ambassador to the team. Consider yourself a public relations spokesperson, and come up with a good response to that fan's question.

- **"Who is the football team's general manager?"** Again, research and preparation will ensure this type of question won't stump you.

- **"Do you take criticism and direction well?"** Like at any job interview, the judges want to see how you describe your weaknesses and whether you can work well with others in a team setting.

- **"Who was our quarterback last season?"** Another research question.

- **"In what ways do you think our sports team can do better this coming season?"** This is similar to an earlier question about the previous season. For this one, you would research what others are saying about the coming season to see if you agree or disagree with the general fan sentiment.

- **"Tell us what you think makes a good leader."** You can name a number of qualities here, so pick the ones that you consider the most important.

- **"What are your favorite charitable causes?"** If you actively volunteer for community causes or participate in marathons and walk events for charity, then this is the time to describe those activities. If you do not personally participate, you can simply talk about the causes that you look forward to working with through the team.

- **"Do you have any hobbies?"** Keep your descriptions short, and share what you like to do for recreation, such as art, sports, classes, or reading.

- **"If there were ever a personal problem between dance team members, what would you do?"** This question tests your maturity, discretion and judgment, as well as your common sense.

- **"If you saw a teammate doing something that was against our rules, what course of action would you take?"** Again, this tests your discretion and judgment.

- **"What is your greatest strength?"** You probably have a number of strengths, so pick one that allows you to describe how that strength will benefit the team.

- **"Tell us how you will balance your outside life with the busy schedule of our dance team promotional and game calendar."** Your answer will vary depending on what your other time commitments are and how you will fulfill all of your obligations.

- **"If you are selected for this team, how do you feel about changing your hairstyle, hair color, or other aspects of your look?"** The team needs flexibility, so will be testing you to see how willing you would be to conform your look to what the team might need.

- **"Professional dancers are often criticized because of how they dress. How would you respond to that criticism?"** You can describe how athletes must wear clothing that allows them to perform at their best, like ice skaters, runners, surfers and ballerinas. Many sports require clothing that would otherwise not be appropriate in other workplaces. In the world of dance, cheerleaders create excitement and drama for the fans by wearing dance costumes designed for maximum freedom of movement and visibility from a distance.

- **"What is your greatest weakness?"** This is a tricky question, but can be successfully answered if you can describe how you control or overcome your weakness, or how your weakness can also have positive effects on your performance.

- **"What would you bring to this team if you make the squad?"** This is essentially your sales pitch for being selected. You should have an answer prepared for this type of question, because the question can come up in various different ways. Even though the way it is phrased might differ, imagine the different ways a judge can ask a question that would be answered the same way as this one.

In conclusion, you should practice answering these and similar questions, but you should NEVER try to memorize answers for any of these word-for-word. You do not want to sound rehearsed or like a script reader. The idea is to sound natural, confident, and well spoken when answering each question. You might get asked three questions, or as many as ten or more. Perhaps you only need to give your introduction, and won't be asked anything additional. There might be two judges, or twelve. You never know what you will encounter, so it is best to prepare for all contingencies.

After the audition

Walking out of the audition room doors will feel GREAT. One way or the other, you did it! You conquered your doubts, fears, and insecurities and showed up with courage. You gave it your all, and lived life fully for the hours you endured the strange and exhausting world of auditioning for a pro dance team.

Sometimes, you will be told whether or not you made the team on the same night as the audition. Other times, a team might announce the results later, such as the next day. So you might walk out of that door knowing whether you made the team, or with some butterflies in your stomach due to the anticipation of finding out whether your tryout resulted in success.

Here are some tips for you, whether you made the team or not.

If you make the team

Congratulations! Your hard work paid off, and luck was on your side as well. Your efforts resulted in your dream coming true, and you can now proudly call yourself a professional cheerleader.

Be sure to comply with any directions from the team as to whether you are allowed to publicly disclose to family and friends that you made it onto the team, or if you have to wait until a certain time or event, such as an announcement on the team website. Your social networking announcements should also comply, so do not post any photos of auditions unless you know you have permission to do so.

Your team director will let you know about any next steps, such as training dates, rehearsal logistics, and schedules. Work hard to be the type of cheerleader that the director can depend on, and be a good role model to everyone around you. Next year, be sure to help another aspiring candidate to live HER dream by serving as a mentor to her!

Best wishes! You are now on your way to one of your life's most exciting adventures!

If you do not make the team

Don't worry, your journey doesn't end there unless you want it to! Show a positive attitude, and do not be bitter or negative about your experience. Like with most job interviews and applications, there are a limited number of spots to fill, and typically, more qualified applicants than the employer can hire show up. In the dance world, you should never take a rejection personally. It is the nature of the business that you will not be selected for everything you audition for; there are just too many dancers out there, and not enough team spots!

If you want feedback, which I encourage you to seek, you can send an email to the team director a week or two after the audition. Include a copy of your application and a photo of yourself to remind the director who you are, and ask if he or she would be willing to give you a few pointers for the following year's audition. Be positive, appreciative for the director's time, and don't be pushy or demanding. In general, it is appropriate to do this only if you made it to the final round.

Remember, this is a tryout based on skill and preparation, but there is also an element of luck. If the cards were not on your side this time, that doesn't mean you would fail again.

The best advice I can give you if this is your dream, is the following: Try out again. And if you have to, again and again. Life is short, but also long. It is too short to wait on the sidelines when you should be pursuing your goals, but also long enough that you can keep at it when a goal proves difficult to reach on the first try. Judge panels rotate, the applicant mix changes, and other factors will be different each year. YOU will change over time as well. So please give yourself another go at it the next year, and if necessary, the year after that, and the year after that, until you achieve your dream.

Chapter 11:
We Are Cheering You On!

Don't just take my advice...

I'm not the only person who wants you to do your best on the day of auditions. In this section, I've included advice, tips, and encouragement from a wide variety of successful arena cheerleader alumni.

These are over 20 of my cheer sisters, many of whom I've shared the field with over the years, cheering you on to success. Let their voices join mine to help you reach your goals! And stay tuned for the next edition of this book, where I will feature even more alumni cheerleaders to mentor you with their advice.

Do you want to be featured in a future edition of this book?

Once you make your dream team, visit the Arena Cheerleader™ Facebook® page at **www.facebook.com/ArenaCheerleader**. Share your success story and favorite success tips in a short wall post. You might be selected to appear in a future Arena Cheerleader™ book or product as a pro cheer alumni mentor!

Melanie Brown

Current Profession:

- Executive Assistant to Warren Moon at Sports 1 Marketing

Pro Teams Melanie has cheered on:

- NFL Seattle Seahawks: Seagals (2 seasons and Pro Bowl Cheerleader)

- NFL San Diego Chargers: Charger Girls (1 season)

Melanie's thoughts on cheering for different teams:

Both teams were incredible experiences. With the Seahawks, I was selected as the Pro Bowl Cheerleader in 2008. I also got to travel to Japan as a representative, as well as to Europe to perform with our Show Group.

With the Chargers, it was amazing to cheer back in my home state of sunny California. Both teams were so different, yet in many ways the same. They were the best experiences of my life!

Melanie's top audition tips:

- SMILE!

- Have FUN!

- Have confidence.

- Don't let others intimidate you, don't worry about them, worry about yourself.

- Put your entire heart into your audition, it will show.

Melanie's favorite cheer memories:

Professional cheering changed my life in so many ways. I grew in my dance abilities, my athleticism, and most of all, my social skills. I was able to meet so many incredible people, make a difference in our community and overseas, and experience so many different cultural experiences while performing overseas. I have made friends to last a lifetime and memories I will never forget.

Melanie's current projects:

I currently work for Hall of Fame Quarterback Warren Moon as his Executive Assistant. I met him while with the Seahawks at a few charity events. He has spun off a Sports Marketing company down in California and I hope to continue to grow my career through his mentoring. The website is **http://sports1marketing.com**.

Sabrina Chaudhry-Ellison

Current Profession:

- NBA Dance Team Director for the Golden State Warriors

Pro Teams Sabrina has cheered on:

- MLB Angels Strike Force: Spirit Team (4 seasons)

- NFL San Francisco 49ers: Goldrush (6 seasons, Captain and Pro Bowl Cheerleader)

- NFL Seattle Seahawks: Seagals (2 seasons, Co-Captain)

Sabrina's thoughts on cheering for different teams:

I think every team has their own signature performance/dance style and overall team look based on the organization's preference and the fan base the team is catering too. In my experience as a dancer on different teams, and even as a coach who has had the opportunity to coach in different states, I would say that's the biggest difference.

Pro Teams Sabrina has coached/directed:

- AFL Spokane Shock Dance Team (I started their first dance team and coached them for 2 seasons)

- NBA Seattle Supersonics Dance Team (2 seasons and then was asked to move to Oklahoma when the team was bought out)

- NBA Oklahoma City Thunder (I started their first dance team and coached them for 2 seasons)

- NBA Golden State Warrior Girls (I am currently in my second season)

Sabrina's top audition tips:

- **Be the Best You!** Judges are looking for individuals who have a "sparkle" and stand out above the rest, so walk into an audition with a positive attitude and have confidence in your abilities.

- **Practice dance!** To be a pro dancer/cheerleader you have to practice your craft. Take dance classes so that you can get comfortable with basic dance technique and learning dance choreography in a sequence. This will make learning the audition routine second nature so that you perform to your best abilities on audition day. You don't want to walk into a pro dance/ cheer audition without any dance training.

- **Learn How to Stand Out!** Teams are looking for someone who stands out and can be the full package- someone who is a dancer, performer, team player and ambassador. This is why I highly recommend taking as many pro dance classes offered by the team you're auditioning for or any outside prep camps like Sideline Ready. These classes give you the exact insight you need to have a competitive advantage. You gain insight and practice ways to stand out at a pro audition from what to wear, how to look, how to perform like a pro dancer and nail the audition interview.

- **Be Fit:** Make sure you're eating healthy, have a good workout regimen and walk into auditions toned and in shape.

- **The Look:** Pro dance is about being glamorous so research the team you're planning to audition for and try to emulate the teams look in terms of hair and make-up.

- **Attire:** Pick an audition outfit that fits your body well and colors that make you stand out. Adding a pop of rhinestones will give you that extra sparkle!

- **Dance Full-out!** When you're at audition ALWAYS dance full-out even when you're learning. I have judged MANY auditions over the years and even when you're learning judges are already taking notes on which dancers stand out as they learn. So it's to your advantage to always dance full out!

Sabrina's favorite cheer memories:

- The first time I was told I made the 49er Goldrush. A dream come true, and my life has forever changed for the better since that moment.

- Hands down the lifetime friends that I have made from being on a pro dance team

- The natural high you got when you step out on the football field to perform in front of a roaring, excited fan base

- Being a Pro Bowl Cheerleader

- Dancing in the Superbowl—Seahawks vs. Steelers

- The opportunity to help start the first Czech Republic Pro Cheer Team—The Eurotel Cheerleaders

- NFL tour to Japan for the American Bowl

Pro dance is a lifestyle and it will forever have a huge impact on my life. I still live and breathe it every day and feel honored that I have been blessed to do so. Through my personal pro dance experience on teams I gained confidence and was pushed to excel as an individual, a leader and as a teammate. In addition, my best friends that I cheered with will be lifelong friends; we went from teammates to being in each other's weddings. We are watching our kids grow up together and now they help judge at my dance auditions. Even though I retired my poms years ago, I walk away rich in friendships and memories.

The experiences shared with my past coaches and teammates have been so impactful on my life that I want to use this next phase of coaching professional dance teams to ensure girls have the same experiences and opportunities I had. I want to share all I have gained with the new talent coming into the pro dance world and my passion lies in cultivating talent, being invested in the growth of my dancers as performers but also as individuals. I work hard to create a positive environment in which my dancers can continue to grow and evolve as individuals and walk away with lifelong friendships, the determination to succeed and understanding the importance of hard work. There's nothing more special than seeing my dancers grow as valuable teammates and young women in the community.

Sabrina's current projects:

I founded Sideline Ready, which is a great resource for those looking to make the jump into the Pro Dance and Cheer industry. Sideline Ready is a collaboration of professional dance team directors, pro dancers, cheerleaders, and sports entertainment producers that know exactly what it takes to cultivate and mentor raw talent to be Sideline Ready. We have guided many professional performers both domestically and internationally on gaining the confidence, look and standout performance quality necessary to be a professional. The website is **www.sidelineready.com.**

Laura (Eilers) Clark

Current Profession:

- Owner, Going Pro Entertainment, LLC

- National Sales Director, Angela King Designs and Go Wild! Wear

- State Director, Miss United States—District of Columbia and Delaware

Pro Teams Laura has cheered on:

- NFL St. Louis Rams: Cheerleaders (1 season)

- NFL Kansas City Chiefs: Chiefs Cheerleaders (5 seasons)

- MLS Kansas City Wizards: Cheerleaders (1 season)

Laura's thoughts on cheering for different teams:

The Rams seemed to be more of a "part-time" job with fewer promotions and rehearsals, and most communication and activities were administered during regularly scheduled practice times. We did not perform full squad routines, so rehearsals were very streamlined—you always performed with your line of five cheerleaders, which made cleaning choreography and learning very simple (yet fun).

The Chiefs included more routines per game and more activities outside of rehearsals, therefore the organization truly became my second family. During the years I was involved, up to six days per week involved pro cheer rehearsals, promotions, hands-on responsibilities in choreography, junior programs, audition clinics and a military variety show.

Both organizations were similar in that the ownership was extremely appreciative of the cheerleading program and the team was very respected in the community.

Pro Teams Laura has coached/directed:

- PIFL (Professional Indoor Football League) Lady Raiders Dance Team of the Richmond Raiders (3 seasons)

Laura's top audition tips:

- Fitness is extremely important. See a personal trainer, get your body fat assessed and work hard. Re-evaluate your diet and be willing to make sacrifices.

- Practice your brief public introduction. Stand with confidence. Speak clearly. Smile. This will most likely be an important part of your audition.

- Think of your audition as your wedding day or prom. Invest in the experience—makeup artist, special attire, and clearing your schedule for the big event.

- False eyelashes will take you from pretty to WOW. They always look great in photos and will make you stand out from a distance.

- Always thank your choreographer, your director, and alumni. Say it sincerely; they don't get told often enough!

Laura's favorite cheer memories:

- Cheering in the loudest stadium in the NFL, a sea of red, when the Chiefs were 13-3 and received a bye into playoffs (2003). Win or lose, it always brought tears to my eyes to hear the national anthem and jets fly over the stadium and know that I was one of the chosen few to represent such a major organization in my hometown of Kansas City.

- We had the special opportunity to bring a taste of home to our U.S. military serving abroad. I especially loved meeting the servicewomen because we had the chance to get to know them and relate to them as female Americans and athletes. Sometimes, we would meet the ladies on the military base for a morning jog before our performances. I visited Mexico, Italy, Germany, Belgium, Egypt, Spain, and Portugal.

Pro cheering shaped me up—physically and mentally! Of course I had the chance to perform professionally for six years for two NFL teams, but there were also two years I did not make my teams: in 2001 as a college graduate auditioning for Chiefs the first time, and in 2008 when I traveled to audition for Dallas Cowboys Cheerleaders.

My first NFL director taught me to be fearless, to be okay with making mistakes, and to embrace criticism which will allow me to be at my very best. This attitude has allowed me to constantly brave new challenges, both professionally and personally.

Laura's current projects:

Based on my unbelievable experiences in pro cheerleading, in 2008, I launched Going Pro Entertainment. We are a network of pro cheer alumni who offer choreography expos, team training, and private audition coaching. We have representatives in nearly every major U.S. market and Canada. The website is **www.goingproentertainment.com**.

Additionally, after I hung up my pom-poms, I found a great performance outlet through pageantry. I was crowned Ms. Virginia United States and then received the national crown as the 2011 Ms. United States. I now direct two state Miss United States pageants: District of Columbia and Delaware. Visit **www.missunitedstates.com** to learn more about this pageant.

Keyna Kirklen Cobb

Current Profession:

- Business Owner/Academic Advisor

Pro Teams Keyna has cheered on:

- NFL San Diego Chargers: Charger Girls (1 season)

- NFL Oakland Raiders: Raiderettes (1 season)

Keyna's thoughts on cheering for different teams:

Each organization has a different fan base. So, when it comes to what to expect out in the community, you have to know whom you are serving. When going from one team to the next, don't expect the same experience as on as your previous team. Do your research so you can be prepared.

Keyna's top audition tips:

- Smile (a lot!)

- Be prepared to perform and to be asked questions outside the box

- Have a plan on what you would do if you made the team (i.e., work, school, family)

- Dance in your tryout uniform ahead of time

- Bring multiple outfits, shoes, nylons, snacks, water, and makeup with you. You never know.

Keyna's favorite cheer memories:

There are too many memories to count! Pro cheering opened my eyes to what real hard work is all about! Pro cheerleading helped me to be prepared for anything and to really LOVE all different kinds of people.

Keyna's current projects:

The idea of developing a community service and event pl. [...] in 2004 shortly after I graduated from Pepperdine Univ [...] Arts in Education—Directing & Training. My reign as Mi [...] 2003 was over, and my third year as a high school teacher v [...] a crossroads for what to do next. So, I started to use my skil [...]iu experiences to build a "special kind" of business. In March of 2011, I launched The Key* Service Company, LLC. Learn all about it at **www.facebook.com/TheKeyServiceCo**.

ollins

ent Profession:

- Director and Instructor for Rhythm Motion (After-School Dance and Cheerleading program)

Pro Teams Kamri has cheered on:

- NFL San Diego Chargers: Charger Girls (2 seasons)

Kamri's top audition tips:

- Dance near the group of "current" girls who are re-trying out (a.k.a. the "vets"). If you can blend in with them, you can show the judges you should be a part of their group/team!

- Have confidence, never show fear, know you CAN make it and belong on the team.

- For the interview, as long as you are smiling and can carry on talking about something... it really doesn't matter what you say or how you answer their question. The judges just want to see if you can speak with confidence and are not afraid to talk to strangers (for example, to possible sponsors at events).

- If you can tumble and/or can speak a different language or have any other talent that will make you stick out from the rest, show it off! Don't hesitate to show off, this is your time to shine and brag ;)

- When it comes to your appearance, wear what they asked you to exactly and then just add a little sparkle. Big hair and red lips are key! When it comes to red lips, stick with a lip stain and not a gloss so your hair doesn't get caught in the stickiness of it, and when it comes to big hair I just mean volume... don't put your hair up! They like it down so you can flip it around! ;)

- On audition day, bring lots of water and snacks... you may not want to eat, but you will need the energy to last throughout the day. It's a long day and you'll want to keep your energy level up!

Kamri's favorite cheer memories:

My first game day is an amazing memory. It was actually my first NFL game, and I felt so blessed, excited, emotional... so many feelings were going through me and I will never forget how I felt that day. I remember I cried during the National Anthem, happy tears. I was just filled with happiness and felt so lucky and happy to be on that field at that moment. Making the team was a very special memory as well, but I'd have to say my first game day was a memory and feeling I will never forget.

Because of my pro cheer career, I met amazing women, friends, and role models. My teammates were all such wonderful women, and I look up to each and every one of them. Not only did I make great friends, but being on the team also made me grow up and mature for the better, which I appreciate greatly. I was only 19 when I made the squad, and being around intelligent professional woman whom I looked up to made me strive to be more like them.

I learned so much on the team. Thanks to our team's "be 15 minutes early" rule, I cannot live without my day planner now! I am now always early for meetings or appointments. I also now know how to put on make-up properly. I have more confidence when it comes to speaking in front of groups of people, thanks to Toastmasters. And I will forever be part of a sisterhood/family that continues to grow every year!

Kamri's current projects:

Charger Girls made me realize how much I love being involved in my community, so I am now a part of the Junior League of San Diego. It also made me realize how much I truly love to dance, teach dance, and be around children (because of my involvement with the Junior Charger Girls program), so I am now working for a former Charger Girls company called Rhythm Motion. It is an after school dance and cheer program that is all over the San Diego and Orange County area. I now get to work with children and teach dance and cheer every day! I'm doing what my passion is, and I can honestly say I love my job! To have a Rhythm Motion class provided at your school, if you live in either the San Diego or Orange County area, contact me at **kamri@rhythmmotion.net** or visit us at **RhythmMotion.net**.

Shelly Cook (Giles)

Current Profession:

- Owner, Salon LG, a full service salon specializing in hair extensions in Solana Beach, CA

Pro Teams Shelly has cheered on:

- NFL San Diego Chargers: Charger Girls (3 seasons)

Shelly's favorite cheer memories:

Cheerleading has had one of the biggest effects on pursuing my life's dreams. I had know idea how much it would affect me until years after being on the field. I have been a dancer my whole life, so when I tried out I was so excited to find an avenue to dance professionally. While I was cheering in '90, '91 and '93, I was also allowed to help other girls get their hair ready for the games. We had a full team of stylists, but I loved doing hair and had about five girls whose hair I would work on, who loved how I did their hair.

Dancing and hair have been my two passions from birth. After college and five years of working in sales, I quit my job and got my cosmetology license. Once I was licensed, I became a stylist for the Charger Girls. Through that experience, I met amazing friends, some of whom are my best friends to this day.

I helped out at games, photo shoots, and did the girls' color and cuts (this was before everyone had hair extensions :)) I have actually stayed closer with the girls whose hair I worked on than the girls who were my teammates from my cheering years.

I am blessed my life went in this direction and I truly believe being a professional cheerleader for the Chargers helped start my path and gave me the confidence to know I could do anything I wanted if I tried hard enough. The first year I tried out in 1990 was the first year Chargers had cheerleaders after 10 years of having no dance team. Over 600 girls tried out and came out from all over the country. When I made the team, that was the beginning of a life of confidence and fulfilling dreams that I hope many other girls who cheer will be able to realize.

Shelly's current projects:

I still dance several times a week and do hair every day. I now own a full service salon, specializing in hair extensions, in Solana Beach, called Salon LG.

Also, about eight years ago, because of my connection with beautiful girls who can dance, I decided to start a burlesque review show called The Lollipop Girls. We performed on a regular basis throughout San Diego for the year I owned the group. After I sold the group to two of my dancers, these girls took the group to a whole other level by creating an amazing show that made it to the finals on the television show, "America's Got Talent."

Tammy McPhee Davila

Pro Teams Tammy has cheered on:

- NFL San Diego Chargers: Charger Girls (2 seasons, including the "first" Charger Girl team)

Pro Teams Tammy has coached/directed:

- NFL San Diego Chargers: Charger Girls (8 seasons)

Tammy's top audition tips:

- Come to the audition prepared. Brush up on your dance technique and turn in a flattering photo of yourself with your application.

- Pre-audition workshops are priceless as a way to get tips from veteran cheerleaders as well as the team director.

- Look and dress your best! Proper make-up application is important.

- If you make it to the finals of the audition: Do your HOMEWORK on the team's organization!!!

- The interview is EXTREMELY important—practice your public speaking and dress professionally! The interview showcases your maturity level.

Tammy's favorite cheer memories:

Being a part of the first Charger Girls team in '90-'91 was very special. I have lifelong friendships from it that I will forever cherish! As a Director, I definitely loved traveling with the team to Australia and shooting the swimsuit calendars in Cabo San Lucas, Mexico.

However, it is so fulfilling to change a person's life and make a positive difference. As a Director, I had the opportunity to serve that role for the women I mentored and coached. That would have to be the most memorable part of the experience for me! The friendships I have made along the way have definitely been the best part.

My experience has affected my life in many ways. As one example, professional cheerleading gave me more confidence to speak in front of large groups of people and on television.

Tammy's current projects:

I am a mother of four wonderful children. I am very active with their school and extracurricular activities. Cheerleading has come full circle for me, as I am now coaching my daughter's cheerleading team. I love my life and believe that all of my experiences have shaped who I am. I feel so blessed to pass on my life lessons and experiences to my children.

Shelly Filippi (Johnson)

Current Profession:

Certified Holistic Health and Nutrition Coach

Pro Teams Shelly has cheered on:

- NFL San Diego Chargers: Charger Girls (2 seasons)

Shelly's top audition tips:

- SMILE :) The absolute most important tip! When I auditioned my first year I was so excited and was performing all out... so much so that I did a turn and leap right into the judges' table (oops!). I kept on smiling and continued on, and I still made the team.

- Eat balanced meals and snacks! Please do not starve yourself to look slimmer in your outfit. You need to fuel your body with proper healthy food to have the energy for the long audition days.

- Look at the current team and notice how they style their hair and do their makeup. The judges want to see if you can fit in with the team.

- Practice what you are going to say when a judge asks "So tell me a little about yourself." You do not want to be tongue-tied, you want to impress them and show them that you are confident and you know exactly who you are.

- Breathe. It sounds obvious, but a lot of girls get so nervous that they look uptight. Take deep breaths and be confident that you are going to be great!

Shelly's favorite cheer memories:

Performing in Sydney, Australia for the NFL American Bowl was pretty fantastic! I have so many memories with all of the girls, and some of them are still my best friends today!

Shelly's current projects:

I am a Holistic Health and Nutrition Coach and founded Living Life Pink **www.livinglifepink.com**.

Living Life Pink specializes in supporting and empowering women to take charge of their health. My goal is to help my clients transform their lives through the power of nutrition, and to encourage them to be the best version of themselves. I am a mom to two young girls and I understand the daily challenge of taking care of yourself amidst a busy life. I teach my clients how to make their health a priority and how to have balance in all areas of their life.

Markéta Formanová

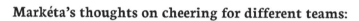

Current Profession:

- On-Air Coordinator (for a TV station in Prague, Czech Republic)

Pro Teams Markéta has cheered on:

- Prague Lions Cheerleaders, Czech Republic (7 seasons)

- Eurotel/O2/Chilli Cheerleaders, Czech Republic (10 seasons, currently Captain)

Markéta's thoughts on cheering for different teams:

The Prague Lions was an American football club—cheerleading was more like "high school" style cheerleading, with all those teenage nice things like ribbons in hair and so on :)

The Chilli Cheerleaders team is more mature, with a more professional approach. It was a "natural evolution" I think—from teenagers to adult ladies!

Markéta's top audition tips:

- Have a positive attitude without any doubts!

- Smile

- Your physical training needs to be adequate to get you to the right fitness level

- You should know everything about the team you are auditioning for— their policy, objectives/targets, history, and motivation

- In all situations, be a professional lady who would perfectly represent the team in every way

Markéta's favorite cheer memories:

- When I first held pom-poms :)

- When I succeeded in auditioning for the Eurotel Cheerleaders team

- Every championship game

- When I was able to return to the team after a lengthy injury in 2007

- When I won the confidence of my teammates and was elected Captain! :)

Cheerleading has changed my life completely. It's not just all those wonderful memories, for which I am grateful, but it also makes me a better person. It always pushes me to try better and harder—and by far I do not mean just physically ;)

Markéta's current projects:

This year I successfully completed a university program focused on aviation, which was my dream—even though I work in a completely different field!

Krystle (Owens) Giordano

Current Profession:

- Certified Nursing Assistant and currently in a Registered Nursing program

Pro Teams Krystle has cheered on:

- NFL San Diego Chargers: Charger Girls (3 seasons)

Krystle's top audition tips:

- Be yourself. You will be nervous, but show your true personality.

- Have fun and show that you really enjoy performing.

- Be professional and respectful.

- Do not compare yourself to other contestants. Think positive and be confident about yourself.

- Show up prepared. Wear the correct attire and shoes. Have you hair and makeup ready. Be on time. Drink plenty of water. Perfect your dance technique.

Krystle's favorite cheer memories:

There was nothing like the first time that I stepped out of the San Diego Charger Helmet with my fellow cheerleaders! The stadium was packed with roaring fans as our players ran through our lines. The excitement gave me goosebumps and I almost cried.

I also loved the opportunity to visit the Navy and Marines off the coast of San Diego. Four of us were picked to go, along with a few players including Drew Brees and Donnie Edwards. What an amazing group of men and woman who have chosen to serve our country! I especially loved the helicopter ride!

I will never forget the friendships I made along the way. I loved our line sleepovers, Christmas and Halloween parties, calendar shoots, and our many hours of practicing as a team.

I remember being told by a veteran cheerleader my first year that this experience will change my life for the better and help me to grow up. I would have to agree. I was only 19 years old when I first made the team. I learned how to be professional and cordial towards my fellow cheerleaders, San Diego Charger staff, the media, and to the fans. We went through an eight-week Toastmasters course where we were taught proper communication skills in front of the media and how to represent our organization in a professional manner. We were expected to wear business attire or our game day attire and always show up 15-30 minutes before any meeting or promotion. This has prepared me for the business world.

Krystle's current projects:

I am currently enrolled in a Registered Nursing program.

Irena Hillbrick

Current Profession:

- Translator (currently on maternity leave)

Pro Teams Irena has cheered on:

- Eurotel Cheerleaders, Czech Republic (5 seasons)

- Chilli Cheerleaders, Czech Republic (formerly the Eurotel Cheerleaders) (1 season)

Irena's thoughts on cheering for different teams:

I have only been on one team, even though it changed its name twice (from the "Eurotel Cheerleaders" it became the "O2 Cheerleaders" in 2005, and then in 2008 it became an independent professional cheerleading team as the Chilli Cheerleaders). But the interesting thing about the team that makes it different from most others is that it does not cheer for one sports team, not even for only one sport. We have cheered for soccer teams, ice hockey teams, basketball teams and many others, during national league games, international games, friendly matches or even important social events.

Irena's top audition tips:

- Prior to the audition attend new dance classes where you learn new choreography often—it helps you not only to get in a better shape physically, but it "exercises" your memory for remembering routines quickly.

- Think positive, try to be in a good mood when you arrive and enjoy the audition as an experience, whatever the outcome—it takes courage to audition, and you have it!

- Have a professional attitude—smile, be friendly, reliable.

- You should know why you want to be on this particular team, and be ready to demonstrate it.

- A cheerleading audition is like a performance, that means appropriate make-up, hair, and clothes.

- Irena's favorite cheer memories:

- Great sports atmosphere at important games with big audiences, and being able to contribute to that atmosphere.

- Traveling with the girls on our bus or in cars to performances in other towns.

- Winning and celebrating a cheer championship.

- Christmas parties and get-togethers with the girls.

- Enjoying dancing to new choreography once it is mastered.

- Many, many others...

Cheerleading has given me confidence, many friends for life, and great memories. I have also enjoyed the dancing!

Irena's current projects:

At the moment, I'm busy trying to live on two continents, and taking care of my young family :-)

Taylor Hooks

Current Profession:

- MRI Technologist

Pro Teams Taylor has cheered on:

- NBA Los Angeles Clippers: Clippers Spirit (5 seasons)

Pro Teams Taylor has coached/directed:

- PASL's Anaheim Bolts

- AIF's Ontario Warriors

Taylor's favorite cheer memories:

I love remembering my first home game of the 2005-2006 NBA Playoffs (vs. Denver Nuggets)—the "sea of red" Clippers shirts and the electric feeling that filled the Staples Center was amazing‼

The friends I made throughout the years are priceless. From the ladies I dance with, to the wonderfully dedicated season ticket holders, to the organization's staff and the Staples Center staff—I am so thankful for the lifelong friends I was lucky enough to make. Having been on a pro dance team gave me the opportunity to be a part of the Sweethearts for Soldiers also—we went to Kuwait a year ago this holiday season to entertain the troops. It was an experience I will cherish every day for the rest of my life.

Karren Kenney

Current Profession:

Criminal Defense Attorney

Pro Teams Karren has cheered on:

- NFL San Diego Chargers: Charger Girls (3 seasons)

- NFL Los Angeles Rams: Cheerleaders (1 season)

Karren's top audition tips:

- SMILE!!!

- If you forget the routine, keep dancing with a smile on your face... don't freak out!

- Depending on the setup—if you get to watch others trying out, CHEER THEM ON!

- Don't dress too revealing or sexy... chances are there are female judges who won't appreciate that.

- During the oral interview, refrain from saying "um" between sentences. You need to sound intelligent and be well spoken.

Karren's favorite cheer memories:

I remember the all-day-long Saturday practices, learning two routines and being completely brain dead by the end of the day. At the opening game for the Chargers in 1991, my skirt fell off in the end zone and my backside was on the BIG screen... LOL!

I loved hanging out with my cheerleader BFF's off the field and taking fun memorable trips.

Professional cheerleading gave me more confidence to appear in front of large groups of strangers and not feel intimidated or shy. I was able to enhance my "performance" skills as a pro cheerleader, and it has turned out to help me immensely in the courtroom. I'm a criminal defense trial attorney, and in order to have a shot at winning a case, you have to be able to perform in front of a jury.

Karren's current projects:

I recently opened my own criminal defense practice in Orange County, California—**http://www.kenneylegaldefense.us**. I'm committed to defending the personal freedom of my clients by making sure the justice system treats them fairly. I handle all types of criminal cases throughout Southern California, with an emphasis in white-collar crime defense.

Tracey Juliana (Holwitz) Lackovich

Current Profession:

President & CEO, Super-Krete International, Inc.

Pro Teams Tracey has cheered on:

- NFL San Diego Chargers: Charger Girls (2 seasons)

- IBL (International Basketball League) San Diego Stingrays (1 season)

Tracey's thoughts on cheering for different teams:

Working with the National Football League is of a much higher caliber. There is a lot more attendance at events, more obvious reasons to be the best ambassador for the team and for the city, much more exposure and more corporate responsibility.

Tracey's top audition tips:

- Wear a color you are most confident in—and don't let it be gray, white or black.

- Don't necessarily get your make-up done for auditions unless you've already had it done before by the same person to your approval. You don't want to be disappointed with your presentation at Go-Time!

- Be in shape—physically AND most importantly, MENTALLY—the choreography may be taught faster than you expect. Make sure your mind is in the right place to learn the material so that when you are up, you can concentrate on giving your best performance instead of remembering the routine.

- Study the dancers prior to auditions to get a feel for the team's style. This could include watching a game, or better yet, attending the pre-audition workshops.

- Be ready to not just make the team, but to COMMIT to the coming year. With rehearsals, appearances, game day, photo shoots, etc., the most difficult part can sometimes be managing your time. It's all worth it in the end, but be prepared to balance your work, school, social life and team life!

- SMILE AND HAVE FUN! Judges not only want to see how well you can dance and perform, but they also watch how you interact with others and will study your overall personality. If you make it through to finals, be prepared to be yourself in answering the toughest questions.

Tracey's favorite cheer memories:

Not only do I cherish the memories I had on the field and in uniform, but I've made best friends for life! Experiencing Charger Girl life with my closest friends and teammates will always be considered part of my most golden moments and my glory days!

Tracey's current projects:

I managed to take over my father's business just before making it onto the Charger Girls and I've been President & CEO ever since. Flavia and I were actually featured in a "Behind the Scenes" Charger Girl television documentary along with teammate Patty Giberson to show the community that Charger Girls are far more talented and skilled than what is demonstrated on the field—though that's plenty in itself!

Should you ever need a concrete facelift, concrete repair, restoration or beautification, call me! **www.super-krete.com**.

Brooke Long

Current Profession:

- Television Host and Cheer Choreographer

Pro Teams Brooke has cheered on:

- NFL San Diego Chargers: Charger Girls (2 seasons)

- AFL (Arena Football League) Los Angeles Avengers: Cheerleaders (1 season)

- NBA Los Angeles Lakers: Laker Girls (3 seasons)

- NBA Miami Heat: Miami Heat Dancers (2 seasons)

Brooke's thoughts on cheering for different teams:

Football fans and stadiums are amazing. Performing at an NFL game is unbeatable. The Charger Girls are some of the sweetest girls I have worked with.

The Laker Girls have a title that holds high expectations. The prestige of this team and recognition is something that I am still proud to be a part of. This team is all about tradition and class. Being based in LA, the Hollywood scene definitely adds to the experience.

The Miami Heat is edgy and spicy. The diversity is unmatched. It was a complete change of pace, focused on hip-hop and style. We took the title from the Laker Girls that year as the "hottest NBA dance team," and the team won the NBA championship.

Pro Teams Brooke has coached/directed:

- I have choreographed routines for pro teams nationwide.

Brooke's top audition tips:

- Personality—have fun, if you look like you are having fun, the judges will have fun watching you.

- Believe in yourself—don't be shy, take the floor with pride.

- Connect: Perform for the judges. Make eye contact throughout your audition.

- Clear speech: Speak loudly and clearly when answering judges. Look at them while you speak and avoid stall words like "ummmmmmm..."

- Wear something that will stand out, it helps them remember you.

Brooke's favorite cheer memories:

Overnight promos are unforgettable. Small towns like Kalamazoo leave a lasting impression. However, nothing can compare to a championship game. Especially when your team wins! I experienced it in Miami and LA, both unforgettable.

I learned so much about myself from pro cheerleading. I gained confidence and learned I was capable of achieving my dreams. Since then, I have exceeded my own expectations. I co-hosted a travel show called *Get Out* and was a model for the hit television show *Deal Or No Deal*. I have appeared on magazine covers and billboards. This all started with pro cheerleading giving me the confidence to follow my dreams.

Brooke's current projects:

See what I am doing now at **www.brookelong.com**.

Andrea Mapes

Current Profession:

- Ambassador at Visalus Sciences

Pro Teams Andrea has cheered on:

- NFL San Diego Chargers: Charger Girls (1 season)

Andrea's top audition tips:

- BELIEVE! First and foremost, you have to believe in yourself, and your dream. I am a huge believer of manifesting your reality! You can have anything you want out of life! Remember as children we believed this to be true whole-heartedly?! Then as we grow and become conditioned, we lose sight of that reality, and we allow FEAR (False Evidence Appearing Real) get in the way. If you want to make a professional dance/cheer team, you must first start with your own mindset! The mind is very powerful. May sound silly, but try this... Actually close your eyes and imagine that very moment when your number is called for the final cut! Visualize yourself in that uniform! Imagine what it would be like to run out on that field! How would this make you feel? Excited? Happy? Accomplished? Do this over and over again! Do this right before you take dance class, before you fall asleep, before you start your day, before you walk into auditions. Do this until your dream becomes a reality.

- SET YOUR GOAL! You must set a clear concise goal for yourself! What exactly are looking to accomplish? Is it to make the team? Is it to advance further in the audition process than you did the previous year? Or is to get the courage to show up? Once you have figured out your goal, write it down!

- DO YOUR HOMEWORK! I would highly recommend researching the team you are auditioning for. What is their team "look"? How are they involved with the community? What is their dance style? You need to educate yourself. Know that you are not only auditioning to be a dancer, but you are also interviewing to be a part of an organization.

- TAKE ACTION! As much as I believe in the power of positive thinking, in order to achieve desired results, your actions must be in direct alignment with your thoughts! You have to put in the physical work! No way around it! Exercise daily to ensure you are in good cardiovascular health. You will need to have the proper endurance to last the duration of long performances. Make sure you are taking dance classes to build on your technique. It's not enough to just "want" to make the team, actually take the time to visualize it. When you goal set, actually write them down. You must take action!

- FOCUS: Make sure to keep a single-minded focus. When audition day arrives, show up looking game-day ready, as if they could put you in the uniform right then and there. Don't allow your fear of "not making it," or your fear of "what others will think," or your fear of "not being good enough" cloud your focus or affect your performance. Dance your heart out and have a blast! Regardless of the outcome this will help you to maximize your experience!

Andrea's favorite cheer memories:

I will never forget that first time running through the tunnel onto the field for team introductions! I remember thinking... "WOW! I did it!"

Dancing professionally in the NFL was an amazing experience and a childhood dream come true! However, I credit the audition process, and all the work I put in leading up the moment they called my number as my true success. I auditioned several times before finally making the team. It is now my story of perseverance! It taught me to never give up, and how to effectively go after what I want in life to get it!

Andrea's current projects:

I promote Life, Health and Prosperity through Visalus Sciences, helping others to live a life by design rather than default! **www.andreamapes.bodybyvi.com**.

Giselle McInnis

Current Profession:

- Financial Analyst / Fitness Studio Co-Owner, barre3

Pro Teams Giselle has cheered on:

- NFL San Diego Chargers: Charger Girls (3 seasons)

Giselle's top audition tips:

- Prepare early! Don't wait until the month of tryouts to pick out an outfit, get in shape, etc. If you try out and don't make the team, think of it as getting an entire year to prepare for the next tryout. Now you know what to expect and what areas you need to improve on!

- Do your research. Each professional team is different. Study the team and figure out what it takes to make that squad. Look for online videos and photos of previous tryouts!

- Work on your "look." Pick a tryout outfit, make-up, and hairstyle that compliments you and makes you stand out from the competition.

- Work on your fitness! Not only for tryouts, but also to make sure your body is prepared for the season if you make the team.

- Have FUN! If you prepare early, that's less you have to worry about. So just have fun and enjoy the tryout process!

Giselle's favorite cheer memories:

Traveling to places such as Mexico City, Hawaii, and Hong Kong with my teammates!

Pro cheering gave me opportunities that I wouldn't have experienced otherwise! It also brought people into my life that I now consider to be a part of my family.

Giselle's current projects:

I am opening up a barre studio, barre3, in San Diego with my best friend and former Charger Girl teammate, Lauren! barre3 combines the grace of a ballet barre with the wisdom of yoga and the strength of Pilates. Our studio will be the first barre3 studio in the state of California!

Lyly Mendez

Current Profession:

- 3-Time Breast Cancer Survivor!

- Entrepreneur, Owner & Designer, Chickie & Smoove Clothing, and Inspiration Point Design Co.

- PROUD Army Wife

Pro Teams Lyly has cheered on:

- NFL San Diego Chargers: Charger Girls (1 season)

- NFL St. Louis Rams: Rams Cheerleaders (5 seasons)

Lyly's top audition tips:

- Practice your public speaking.

- Practice your technical dance skills.

- Be aware of the beauty and appearance attributes of the team you're auditioning for. There are differences depending on what area of the country your team is located in. (i.e., when I was cheering for the Rams, we all wore the same color red lipstick. Some teams prefer a specific hairstyle, lots of volume and lift versus sleek, etc. Some teams are more conservative, believe it or not!) If the judges see that you took the time to research the minutiae like that, you'll score points!

- Do your research on the players, their positions, their stats, and most importantly, their philanthropic efforts. These things can help you form an opinion about the team, which will help you answer the question THAT IS ALWAYS ASKED, "why do you want to be a _____ Cheerleader?"

- If you can go, definitely attend the pre-audition workshop, or hire an audition coach.

Lyly's favorite cheer memories:

Cheering in Super Bowl XXXIV and being on the winning team!! Being a part of USO Tours. Making lifelong friendships.

Pro cheering helped to make me a well-rounded individual. It gave me an opportunity to do things I would have never had a chance to do. It opened my mind to things I had no clue about before being an NFL Cheerleader.

Lyly's current projects:

I am an entrepreneur. I own two clothing companies with my husband, Chickie & Smoove Clothing and Inspiration Point Design Co.

Chickie & Smoove Clothing is an e-commerce clothing store where we sell graphic t-shirts that I design with my husband. **www.chickieandsmoove.com**.

Inspiration Point Design Co. is also an e-commerce clothing store, but at IPDco we allow our fans to be the designer. They come to us with a design idea and we make it happen for them... on t-shirts, bags, scarves, whatever! **www.inspirationpointdesign.co**.

Ashley Monzon

Current Profession:

- Personal Trainer, High School Cheer Coach & High School Dance Coach

Pro Teams Ashley has cheered on:

- NFL San Diego Chargers: Charger Girls (6 seasons)

Ashley's top audition tips:

- My number 1 tip to anyone is to simply HAVE FUN! The judges are looking for women that are enjoying themselves, making the judges have fun too!

- Show your personality. Most teams don't want the cookie cutter dancer, they are looking for women who are confident in who they are as individuals.

- Look online at the respective team's current team. Find someone that has similar features as yourself, then do your best to replicate that person's look. I know I said to be yourself, but you also need to be able to fit in to what the team's needs are with regard to your looks!

- Act as if you are already on the team. Show the judges that you know how to carry yourself in interviews and also with other individuals. Someone is always watching.

- Lastly, this one is more geared to your dancing. Copy the style as best as possible. Remember, you are auditioning for a team, not a solo dance performance. Usually, the choreographer works with the actual team so don't overdo it with your own style! Yes, you want to stand out with your personality, but do the choreography in a way that fits in!

Ashley's favorite cheer memories:

There are so many to choose from. I was very lucky to perform at multiple playoff games, and travel to Japan, Guam and Hawaii on an AFE Tour. But no memory tops the feeling I had getting ready to run out of the tunnel at my very FIRST game. I was 18 years old, and I can remember waiting under the stands, listening to the fans cheer for the start of the game, and thinking to myself, "Wow, I am a professional NFL Cheerleader! How did I get so lucky?" That happened in the summer of 2002, and to this day, I still get chills thinking about that excitement running through my bones!

Cheering for the Chargers helped shape me into who I am today. At 18 years old, I had no clue what I was going to do with my life. I had never been out of the country and I was incredibly shy. My Charger Girls experience helped me come out of my shell, taught me how to speak publicly, and gave me the confidence to start my own personal training business. The women I met throughout the years had amazing talents and they taught me to be strong for what I believe in, have faith in the unknown, and truly know what it means to be a friend.

Ashley's current projects:

Currently, I coach high school cheer and dance with the hope to teach young girls not only how to cheer and dance, but more importantly, life lessons.

I also run my own in-home personal training business. I specialize in weight loss and toning. I believe health is a way of life and that before you can be healthy, you must believe you are healthy. I teach women's "bootycamps" all over San Diego, where I show ladies not only how to work out, but also how to live a healthy lifestyle WITHOUT dieting. My philosophy is simply "Shape your mind. Shape your body." My website is **www.ashleymonzon.com**.

I am also working with Flavia to create fitness training specifically geared for the current or aspiring arena cheerleader. Stay tuned! And be sure to join the mailing list at **www.ArenaCheerleader.com** to be the first to hear about the program.

Martina Němcová

Current Profession:

- Cheer Academy instructor, Chilli Dancers instructor (currently on maternity leave)

Pro Teams Martina has cheered on:

- Prague Lions Cheerleaders, Czech Republic (11 seasons)

- Eurotel/O2/Chilli Cheerleaders, Czech Republic (8 seasons)

Martina's thoughts on cheering for different teams:

The Prague Lions was more of a sports cheer squad belonging to an American football team. Performances included a lot of stunts, chants and short routines. It was cheerleading for younger girls (mostly high school age). Chilli Cheerleaders is a semiprofessional team that pays more attention to the image of the girls—their beauty and grace, and it focuses on the uniqueness of the team in the Czech Republic and uses various dance styles. It is only for women aged 18 years and older.

Pro Teams Martina has coached/directed:

- Prague Lions Cheerleaders, Czech Republic (11 seasons)

- Chilli Cheerleaders, Czech Republic (5 seasons)

- Chilli Dancers, Czech Republic (2 seasons)

Martina's top audition tips:

- Be positive (be friendly, smile).

- Be optimistic (enjoy the experience).

- Be prepared (your appearance, your clothes, your make-up).

- Find out about previous auditions for the team, so you have an idea about what to expect.

- If you're not great at speaking and expressing yourself in front of people, practice it so you can be confident on the day of auditions.

Martina's favorite cheer memories:

There are a lot of them, but first comes in my head our first championship outside of the Czech Republic, and also my first cheer training camp in Germany (1995), where I was surprised how much behind we are in the Czech Republic :-)

Pro cheerleading has affected my life in so many ways. Now I have a husband and two children, but I am still actively involved in cheerleading. I would actually love to stay involved as long as possible and make it my main source of income. Even my older daughter has started attending cheerleading lessons this year :-)

Martina's current projects:

In 2012, I and two women (Chilli Cheerleader's coach Olga Koprivova along with another former Chilli Cheerleader and choreographer, Andrea Novackova) founded the Cheer Academy in Prague—a school for girls aged 4-16 that teaches cheerleading basics as well as other dance styles and gymnastics. The goal is to give the girls a well-rounded physical education program and inspire them to pursue cheerleading. I am on maternity leave now, but I work by being a dance instructor at the Cheer Academy and also at Vesely Certik, a family club, both in Prague. The website for the Cheer Academy is **www.cheeracademy.cz**.

The other project that just started is a dance team for "retired" Chilli Cheerleaders, who can no longer be active cheerleaders for family or scheduling reasons, but still love dancing very much and want to keep seeing each other and dancing. It's called the Chilli Dancers, and at the moment consists of twelve dancers, some of whom already have families. I coach and choreograph for that dance team. The website is **www.cheerleaders.cz**.

Lindsay Rizzo

Current Profession:

- Full-time salesperson in Reverse Mortgages and Personal Development

Pro Teams Lindsay has cheered on:

- NFL San Diego Chargers: Charger Girls (2 seasons)

Lindsay's top audition tips:

- Try, try, try and try AGAIN!! It took me four auditions to finally make the squad. I stayed focused on my goal and every time made small improvements to my look, techniques, and overall knowledge of what judges are looking for. Truth is...You never know!! So if you have a dream or a goal of making the squad, stay focused on that and one day your day will come true.

- Stay connected: Keep in contact with anyone you know who is on the team or involved in the organization you wish to be a part of. Things are constantly changing and being in the know with any new information is great!

- GO TO THE WORKSHOP!! In my eyes, it was not my "dance skills" that were preventing me from making the squad, so I never attended the workshops most teams offer. The year I finally went to an audition workshop, I received some great feedback on what to wear, make-up, hair, etc. Sometimes it is the things we have not thought of that are important!!

- Judges are always watching... So bring your "A GAME." The audition process, whether you know it or not, starts from the moment you send in your application! If you are serious about making a team, be prepared... have a good headshot and a great resume. On audition day, act as if the whole day is an audition... they are watching! Go FULL OUT every time, leave nothing on the dance floor, and really give it all you've GOT!

- Be patient, be kind, be YOU!! We as women and dancers can get so focused on "what they are looking for"... the truth is that sometimes they do not even know. SO BE YOU! No really... bring the best YOU to the table on audition day. Be authentic in the interview, be the WOMAN that you want to represent all year long... when it is your time, you will know... I DID!!

- Most importantly, never give up! If you truly are passionate for the right reasons about being on a team, then go for it! You decide what you want and wait for the rest to fall into alignment with that desire!!

Lindsay's favorite cheer memories:

My very first moment of running out of the tunnel was the most amazing experience EVER! I had never been to a PRO football game, so to be on the field, see the thousands of FANS cheering, and being able to achieve one of my dreams... was PRICELESS!!

Being a part of the Chargers organization / San Diego Charger Girls was a HUGE eye opener to the fact that being a "public figure" comes with responsibility. Many young women set out on this dream for the glamour of wearing the uniform. For me... being in that uniform meant representing something SO MUCH BIGGER than myself. Being outward focused at fundraisers, events and games meant truly being the best ME I knew how to be! While it was always my dream to be a professional dancer, what I learned was that giving back to the community means SO much more!

The biggest thing I can say about my time with the Charger Girls is... I will never forget the amazing moments that were created on and off the field. I am forever grateful for the friendships I formed being a part of that organization. I am now a wife and mommy to two beautiful little girls. I look forward to the days when I will tell my girls what Mommy did and show them pictures of my fond memories! It was a dream that I had for many years and finally came true! I truly believe in the team's saying... "Once a CG...ALWAYS a CG."

Lindsay's current projects:

I recently won the title of Mrs. Corona Del Mar 2013!

I am a believer of serving others first and being grateful for what we have in order to really go out and ACHIEVE success!! I carry that over into my professional work in Personal Development.

Alexis A. Rodriguez

Current Profession:

- Admissions Operations Coordinator for Ashford University

Pro Teams Alexis has cheered on:

- NPSFL (National Public Safety Football League) San Diego Enforcers: Enforcer Girls (4 seasons and currently also Dance Director)

- ABA (American Basketball Association) San Diego Surf: Surfettes (1 season)

- ABA (American Basketball Association) San Diego Wildcats: Dance Team (1 season)

- NIFL (National Indoor Football League) San Diego Shockwave: Lady Shakers (1 season)

- AFL (Arena Football League) San Diego Riptide: Dance Team (1 season)

Alexis's thoughts on cheering for different teams:

Before directing the San Diego Enforcer Girls, I was on four other minor league dance teams here in San Diego. My main observation is that with the Enforcer Girls, the organization makes it clear that it appreciates all of our hard work. On the other teams, we were not always aware of who was running the organization nor was there as much recognition for what we do as cheerleaders, so this varies from team to team.

Pro Teams Alexis has coached/directed:

I am the creator and dance director for the San Diego Enforcer Girls. I created this team with my twin sister Angela in 2010.

Alexis's top audition tips:

- Have fun

- Smile

- Wear red lipstick

- Avoid wearing shorts and stick with a black brief

- If you happen to mess up, keep going and smiling as if nothing wrong ever happened!

Alexis's favorite cheer memories:

I enjoyed creating the first Enforcer Girls swimsuit calendar. I enjoyed every second of the making from selecting which swimsuits the ladies would wear, to selecting the cover shot, then planning the calendar release party. It was a spectacular project. A portion of the proceeds of our calendar go right back to our charity of choice, United Cerebral Palsy. Creating a swimsuit calendar is an event that I now look forward to making every season.

Being a professional cheerleader has given me an opportunity to be more involved in my community. There have been several news segments I was involved with, and I participate in many fundraisers. Most importantly, I have had the honor to meet some of my best lifelong friends. Cheering at my age allows me to achieve a work-life balance in my life. I love that I can still do what I am passionate about and make a positive change in the community where I live.

Alexis's current projects:

I love dance, and have performed with West Coast Cabaret and the Olio Show, both in San Diego. I am currently training with my sister to run my first marathon, San Diego's Rock & Roll marathon, in 2013.

Angela A. Rodriguez

Current Profession:

- Student Services Manager for Ashford University

Pro Teams Angela has cheered on:

- NPSFL (National Public Safety Football League) San Diego Enforcers: Enforcer Girls (4 seasons and currently also Dance Director)

- ABA (American Basketball Association) San Diego Surf: Surfettes (1 season)

- ABA (American Basketball Association) San Diego Wildcats: Dance Team (1 season)

- NIFL (National Indoor Football League) San Diego Shockwave: Lady Shakers (1 season)

- AFL (Arena Football League) San Diego Riptide: Dance Team (1 season)

Angela's thoughts on cheering for different teams:

Before directing the San Diego Enforcer Girls, I was on four other minor league dance teams here in San Diego with my twin sister, Alexis. The fans, organization and community really have a high level of respect and admiration for the Enforcer Girls. Other teams I have danced for didn't give their dance teams as much recognition. All of the women that I have danced with are hard working women that have a true passion for dancing and being involved in the community.

Pro Teams Angela has coached/directed:

I am the creator and dance director for the San Diego Enforcer Girls. I created this team with my twin sister Alexis in 2010.

Angela's top audition tips:

- Smile

- Wear dramatic eyelashes to make your eyes stand out

- Wear red lipstick

- Avoid wearing shorts and stick with a black brief

- If you happen to be rejected never be afraid to try again

Angela's favorite cheer memories:

Like my sister also said, I really enjoyed creating the first Enforcer Girls swimsuit calendar. I enjoyed the entire process. All of the women were so dedicated in preparing for our first calendar, and they all inspired my sister and me to make this the best calendar it can be. A portion of the proceeds from our calendar goes to charity, which is great.

Being a professional cheerleader has given me the opportunity to pursue my passion to dance and perform in front of some of the most amazing and loyal fans. I have established many lifelong friendships along the way, and appreciate the community involvement opportunities available to me.

Angela's current projects:

I was a performer in the West Coast Cabaret and the Olio Show with my sister, Alexis. We are both training to run the San Diego Rock & Roll marathon in 2013.

Brooke Michael Russo (Bennett)

Current Profession:

- Sales Manager in San Diego for Toll Brothers, Inc., America's Luxury Homebuilder

Pro Teams Brooke has cheered on:

- NFL San Diego Chargers: Charger Girls (3 seasons)

Brooke's top audition tips:

- Doll up. Sounds very silly, but big pretty hair and bold/stage makeup help because it helps them imagine you in the part. Wear dance briefs (Capezio) and Capezio tan dance tights underneath or just Sheer Energy tan nylons. Wear a jazzy and flattering sports bra or halter-top, and halter style is best. Wear jazz shoes instead of sneakers.

- Dress like a dancer, not like a cheerleader. At my first audition, I showed up thinking "sporty" and was totally the odd man out... I wished I had red lipstick on and poufy hair.

- Check the website. They post workshop dates in advance. There is usually a small fee, but the workshops give you two advantages: a comfort level with the material and the style that you'll see at the audition, and a chance to network with the team director to ask questions.

- Pack food and water. It will be a very long day... Drink lots of water. The dancers are on their feet all day so be sure you are prepared.

- Be up to speed with current events. The interview process is grueling and it's important to show that you know what's going on in the world, in the country, city, organization and with the league.

- Wear dance shoes, not sneakers. (Again back to my "sporty" attempt gone wrong).

- SMILE—I know you know how... but they watch how the girls interact with one another and if they are pouty or unfriendly even while off stage, they can take that into account. They want a team of professional, mature dancers who will get along seamlessly. Bring only happy faces. And display showmanship even while practicing. Show them you are fun‼ They want fun team players‼‼ ;0)

- Practice picking up new material. For the best chance, take a few classes (anywhere new) so that you have the opportunity to pick up new material at a fast pace. They move through the material very quickly and that's what makes a lot of girls get overwhelmed. They give you time to practice after teaching material before they make you go in front of the judges. Knowing that should help calm the nerves as you're learning.

- Don't freak out. The veterans who are trying out again get added into the mix during auditions (on most teams, veterans reaudition every year, and yes, girls who were on the team the previous year can get cut). The veterans come in looking all perfect and intimidating... when I saw them for the first time, my jaw dropped and I began stressing. They knew to come "game-day ready" and I had NO IDEA, so again, I stress that you should really play the part. Theater make-up is perfect... put on black eyeliner, blush, and red lipstick. I swear it helps... even fake lashes (but only if you've worn them before). Rat that hair, rat it, rat it, rat it‼ ;0)

- Practice turns and leaps. Double-turns at least, and axels if you have them. If you don't know how to perform turns, showmanship can make up for a lot.

- Here's a little secret... Don't look around at the other people dancing with you when it's down to dancing in small groups of two or three. Remember, someone could mess up—so you don't want to be watching her and mess up too! If you do mess up, just smile and move on... They want to see that you can handle the stress and the eyes on you. If there's a mistake, it's not the end of the world.

- Don't get discouraged. My cousin Brian is the person who convinced me to audition. He begged me to go, and it was truly a lot of fun. I left all PUMPED even though I didn't make it the first year I tried out! So keep trying. I left that first time just stoked that I got to learn cool dances from amazing choreographers (and knowledge of what to do better next time). Worst thing that can happen is that you spend a day in a gym getting an awesome dance workout. It's really fun. Remember, this is a job interview and a dance lesson, not a cutthroat competition... it is a professional organization where everyone is kind and welcoming. You will leave with a great experience under your belt no matter how it pans out.

- Repeat this mantra to help you stay motivated: "Free tickets to every home game!!!"

Brooke's favorite cheer memories:

- Traveling to Australia (our) rookie year to perform at the American Bowl!

- Singing the opening National Anthem for the game with fellow Charger Girl, Coreena Mulloy.

- Participating in the inaugural Junior Charger Girl Camp / Fundraiser & Half Time Show... which continues to raise funds for various charities.

- Being on the sidelines for my hometown team!

- The swimsuit calendar photo shoots will always be great memories as well, especially having the good fortune to make the cover one year!

- My most unforgettable memory was when I fell down in front of 60,000+ fans at a Charger game versus Denver!

Brooke's current projects:

I spend much of my personal time behind the lens doing portrait photography. You can find me on Facebook as "Brooke Russo Photography."

I have been selling real estate and representing large publicly traded homebuilders since early 1999. Currently, I am a Sales Manager in San Diego for Toll Brothers, Inc., **www.TollBrothers.com**.

Jessica Vorpahl

Current Profession:

- Project Manager at a Design Agency

Pro Teams Jessica has cheered on:

- NBA Minnesota Timberwolves: Timberwolves Dancers (2 seasons)

- International Hip Hop Team "Exisdanz" (World Champs in Hip Hop) (1 season)

Jessica's top audition tips:

- Smile & show personality!

- Be confident

- Don't be afraid to dance outside your shell

- Dress/act the part

- Have a positive attitude at all times

Jessica's favorite cheer memories:

Some favorite cheer memories are getting ready in the locker room, playing all of our favorite hit songs from the year and dancing around while we got ready. I also loved one of our appearances. We traveled to North Dakota and performed at a minor league basketball team. It was a fun weekend with some of the girls dancing at half time, meeting new people, signing autographs, and touring a small town in North Dakota.

Pro cheer/dance has forever changed my life. First, I went from blonde to brunette for my "look," for which I am forever grateful. I love my new brunette color. I now have more confidence to tackle other dance positions, coaching, choreographing, and trying new dance opportunities. It's also changed my personal life. I have 25-30 close girlfriends that I will be connected with for life. It has brought me some of my best friends and best experiences.

Jessica's current projects:

Currently, I am a project manager at a design agency. It's called KNOCK, **www.knockinc.com**.

I'm also coaching a high school dance team and planning a wedding. It's quite an exciting time!

Chapter 13:

What's Your Motivation?

You can do it! You really can!

In the end, we feel the most accomplished when we achieve difficult goals. A pro dance team audition requires dancing under the scrutiny of judges, public speaking in front of panels of critical eyes, and grooming yourself into a Hollywood-worthy version of yourself. This is no small feat, and not for the faint of heart.

Going through with it will be one of the most courageous acts of your life, no matter what the outcome.

We regret the things we didn't do more than the things we did. This is true of life. Please don't let this opportunity live in the "should have" box; make it a bucket list item that gets checked off! Do it while you can, as a celebration of your ability to live deeply and fully.

As one of my favorite mentors, Brendon Burchard, wrote in his book, *The Charge:*

> "[I]n selecting your next challenge in life, choose one that is meaningful... great challenges stretch our efforts and capabilities, demanding slightly more than the best of our skills and strengths. They are just over and above our current abilities, so they require us to fully engage... and grow."

And I'd like to also quote one of my favorite speeches, given by Theodore Roosevelt in 1910:

> "It is not the critic who counts; not the man who points out how the strong man stumbles, or where the doer of deeds could have done them

better. The credit belongs to the man who is actually in the arena, whose face is marred by dust and sweat and blood; who strives valiantly; who errs, who comes up short again and again... who at the best knows in the end the triumph of high achievement, and who at the worst, if he fails, at least fails while daring greatly, so that his place shall never be with those cold and timid souls who know neither victory nor defeat."

We were all put on this planet to face challenges, and to meet those tests with the best that we can summon from within. As infants, we took our first steps, without asking whether we should be afraid of change and growth. As children, we welcomed learning and difficulty with an eager eye and ready mind. Now, as adults, we need to continue on that journey of growth, always. We need to seek new ground to walk on, and new skills to master. We need to be visionaries and goal setters, but more importantly, we need to take action toward those dreams, always taking those first steps into whatever new territory we set out to explore.

If your journey includes a career in professional arena cheerleading, nobody can take the first steps but you. They are your feet, so get out there and *dance*!

Even though this book is about becoming a professional cheerleader, I hope that the message is larger than that. My core message is about dreams, and action, and living your life fully. If you have a dream, get that dream out of your head and into your life by taking action. Make it an accomplishment, not just a vision. Make it your *life*, not just an unrealized goal.

I hope that my words in this book, the words of others quoted above, and the words of the pro cheer alumni featured in these pages have helped you find the inspiration to pursue this amazing goal.

I truly honor you for your vision and bravery, and I send you my blessings.

Much love,
Flavia

What next?

If you love this book, please don't forget to leave a review at **Amazon.com**. It really means a lot to get feedback from you, the reader. I read every single review. Every single one, without fail. Success stories are the best of all!

You can also send me a personal email through the website at **www.ArenaCheerleader.com**.

On the website, you can access the "book extras" downloads and join the free mailing list to periodically receive:

- Choreography videos

- Tips & tricks

- Audition news

- Interviews with current pro cheerleaders

- Spotlight articles on team directors

- Announcements about new books and editions

- Info about retreats and bootcamps

- Discounts from companies who want you to try their makeup, nutrition, and other products

- Healthy recipes

- News and articles about the pro cheer world

Thanks again for purchasing this book and good luck at auditions!

Cheers!

Made in the USA
Coppell, TX
12 March 2022

74886859R00109